BARRON'S

U.S. CITIZENSHIP TEST

BARRON'S

U.S. CITIZENSHIP TEST

8TH EDITION

Gladys E. Alesi, M.B.A.
Executive Director (Retired)
American Immigration and Citizenship Conference

Former Consultant to the
Department of Justice,
Immigration and Naturalization Service

Former Administrator of English and
Citizenship Program of
New York City Board of Education

BARRON'S

About the Author:
Gladys E. Alesi's first teaching assignment was to teach English and citizenship to refugees of the Holocaust at Public School 80 in Brooklyn, New York. After a succession of promotions, she became administrator of the English and Citizenship Program of the New York City Board of Education. She also served as Executive Director of the American Immigration and Citizenship Conference and as a consultant to the Department of Justice, Immigration and Naturalization Service.

Updated forms and information provided by *Leya B. Speasmaker, MT, MPA, MA*, Field Support Coordinator/ESL Specialist, Catholic Legal Immigration Network, Inc. (CLINIC), Washington, DC.

All inquiries should be addressed to:
Barron's Educational Series, Inc.
250 Wireless Boulevard
Hauppauge, New York 11788
www.barronseduc.com

Library of Congress Control No.: 2013940522

ISBN: 978-1-4380-0218-7

Printed in the United States of America
9 8 7 6 5 4 3 2

10%
POST-CONSUMER
WASTE
Paper contains a minimum of 10% post-consumer waste (PCW). Paper used in this book was derived from certified, sustainable forestlands.

This is the Flag of the United States of America.

If you are a U.S. citizen, this is <u>your</u> flag.

If you want to be a U.S. citizen, you can be <u>naturalized</u>.

This book will tell you how to prepare for the test.

Contents

PART THREE—PREPARING FOR THE TEST

LIST OF CHARTS AND ILLUSTRATIONS

Introduction

Are you ready to prepare yourself for your naturalization test? Use this book! This book has many practice exercises and tests to help you develop the skills and knowledge needed for the interview. It contains sample questions, some of the forms required, and information on how to obtain other forms that you may need.

What it does *not* contain is legal advice for applicants with special legal problems. Those with questions about eligibility, entry, status, a criminal record, and so on, should seek professional help before they file. Professional help is available from private immigration attorneys or from Board of Immigration Appeals (BIA) recognized agencies and accredited representatives. A listing of BIA recognized agencies and accredited staff can be found at *www.justice.gov/eoir/ra/raroster.htm*.

Be careful to obtain legal advice only from people who are authorized to provide it. There are many people, such as *notarios*, who say they can help you but who do not know what they are doing. They will charge you a lot of money and may cause big problems with your application.

This book will help prepare you for the citizenship test. To pass the test, you must be able to follow the directions given to you by the interviewer and to answer questions about your application. You must also pass the civics, writing, and reading portions of the test. You must be able to write correctly one sentence dictated to you by the interviewer. You will have three opportunities to do this correctly. You must be able to read out loud one sentence given to you by the interviewer. You will have three opportunities to do this correctly. The reading and writing portions of the test use the vocabulary provided by USCIS, and these lists are included on pages 189 and 191 of this book. Finally, you must be able to answer six out of ten of the civics questions given to you by the interviewer. These questions are included in this book starting on page 195.

All of the preparation materials in this book are in accordance with present immigration law. At this time (2013), changes to immigration law are being contemplated by the United States Congress. Immigration forms are often updated. It is very important that you check on the United States Citizenship and Immigration Services (USCIS) webpage (*www.uscis.gov*) for the most current information and forms.

A LETTER FROM THE AUTHOR

Welcome,

You already have a green card; you are 18 years of age or older; you have entered the country legally. Now you are ready to go on. Welcome to "A Nation of Immigrants," joining others who believe in freedom and justice. It is time for you to participate in your new country as an American citizen!

A citizen has many rights and privileges. A naturalized citizen has all the rights of a native-born citizen except for one, and that is, a naturalized citizen can never become president or vice president of the United States—every other job may be a possibility! A naturalized citizen has responsibilities, too. They include loyalty to the United States, its Constitution, and its laws.

I know how hard you must work to go from alien to citizen. I know you can do it, and I know you will be a good citizen.

Sincerely,

Gladys Alesi

Gladys Alesi

ACKNOWLEDGMENTS

I gratefully acknowledge the kindness of those concerned with granting permission to reprint passages, charts, and drawings. Special appreciation is offered to the U.S. Departments of Justice and Homeland Security, whose descriptive drawings, charts, and sample test (which has been expanded and adapted) have helped to enhance this publication. Without the help of my daughter, Catherine A. McCollum, I could never have brought this guide to conclusion. Her unfailing empathy and support combined with her research assistance made this edition possible.

HOW TO USE THIS BOOK

This is a workbook. That means you must work all the exercises in the order they are presented. You must follow the instructions if you want to succeed.

READ 1 TO 6 aloud to a friend or in front of a mirror.

1. I am at least 18 years old. I am _____ years old.
2. I was legally admitted for permanent residence.

3. I have resided here for at least five years, unless I qualify for an exception (see page 15).

4. I am a person of good moral character.

5. I am willing to take an Oath of Allegiance to the United States of America.

6. I am learning to speak, read, and write English. I am learning all about the history, geography, and government of my new country.

When you are alone, practice saying the above as many times as you can!

This book has three parts:

PART ONE—called BECOMING A U.S. CITIZEN

Read about the flag, and then do all the reading exercises. Put a line under a word you do not understand, and look it up in the Word List at the back of the book.

PART TWO—called APPLYING FOR U.S. CITIZENSHIP

Obtain the application form (N-400). Practice filling in the blanks on the form, in pencil. Check the instructions.

File your application, with fees and everything needed, and WAIT.

Appear for the interview at the time and place you are told. Answer every question slowly and thoughtfully.

Take the Oath of Allegiance.

PART THREE—called PREPARING FOR THE TEST

Do all of the reading and writing exercises and study for the American government, history, and geography questions. The questions and answers are in the reading exercises, and they are also in the back of the book.

NOTE: This is a self-help book. While you are learning important facts, each unit aims to help you improve your English. Pay attention to words and their meanings.

Each part is explained in great detail in this book. Check the Contents now.

READ ABOUT TESTS

There are many tests in this book. They provide the practice you need. Another word for test is *quiz*. Some of the short tests are called *reviews*. A review means "a systematic study of something just learned." Take all the tests, even those that seem difficult at first. You will gain confidence as you do them again and again. Look ahead to the time you can discuss them as a citizen!

PART ONE

BECOMING A U.S. CITIZEN

Looking Ahead

As you learn about the government and history of your new country, you will also improve your English language skills, that is, if you follow all the instructions. You will be given reviews so that you are well prepared when the time comes for you to take the Oath of Allegiance to your new country!

Practice makes perfect! That old saying tells you how to do it. Reading and answering questions about what you have read will help. Get a local newspaper to read, and try to make up your own questions about what you have read. Put a line under words you don't understand. Find out what they mean by asking a neighbor, by looking up the word in the Word List in the Appendix, or by using a dictionary. Most important, take all of the tests in this section. Whenever you can, read them out loud. Do each exercise several times. Follow the instructions each step of the way.

Now, turn the page and read about the American flag. Answer the questions about it. You may hear a question about the flag at your naturalization examination. You are looking ahead to American citizenship—it takes time and work. Take the first step.

THE FLAG

Another word for flag is *banner*. The national anthem is the "Star-Spangled Banner." Another word for anthem is *song*. Sometimes the flag is called Old Glory.

Now read this poem about the flag and answer the questions about it.

America Is Her Flag

Fifty stars are in her flag
for the 50 states in her Union.
June 14, 1777, the flag of the United States of America
had 13 stars—one for each state in the new Union.

This flag had 13 stripes,
a ribbon for each of the first colonies.

And poets say the colors in our flag
stand for the things we hold dear—
red for courage,
white for truth,
blue for honor.

A country is as strong as its ideals.

We love the things for which Old Glory stands.

You can help hold these colors high.

Figure 1

Source: U.S. Department of Justice, Immigration and Naturalization Service

1. What are the colors of the American flag? _____

_____

2. What do the colors stand for? _____

_____

3. Why does the flag have 13 stripes? _____

_____

4. Why does the flag have 50 stars? _____

_____

5. What is the national anthem (song)? _____

_____

See the answer key on page 181.

Reading Practice Exercises

You may have read some general information about citizenship in the United States. Now you will read more, with exercises for reading comprehension.

There are six reading exercises and a summary. Do them in order—the first, second, and so on—answering the questions before you go to the next passage. Check your answers with those on pages 181–185. Do not give up until they are all correct!

Now, begin with reading exercise 1. Follow instructions. Read aloud so you will become familiar with the sounds of English.

Practice your English by reading the passage below in front of a mirror or have someone listen to your pronunciation. Then answer the questions.

1. IMMIGRATION

From earliest times, people have migrated (moved) from one place to another. When the first colonists came to this land in the 1600s, they worked hard to settle and build a great country. Since that time, about 40 million settlers have come and been welcomed here.

Records of immigrants were first kept in 1820. For that year, the number of immigrants was about 8,000. This number grew steadily and by the middle of the 1800s, it increased 10 times. By the end of the century (1899), the first laws against "free immigration" were in effect.

Congress has since made laws to control the number of aliens coming to this country as immigrants. In 1986, the Immigration Reform and Control Act (IRCA) was created to legalize aliens who had lived here, worked here, or who came here to join their families.

The most recent large-scale immigration law is the Illegal Immigration Reform and Immigrant Responsibility Act (IIRIRA) of 1996, passed by Congress and signed by President Bill Clinton. This book is in agreement with both of these laws, which are reflected in the Immigration and Naturalization Act.

REVIEW

Now write the answers to these questions in the spaces provided.

1. What does migration mean?_____

_____

2. About how many immigrants have come here from the 1600s to

the present?_____

3. What is a recent immigration law?_____

4. When was the first immigration law passed? _____

5. When did the first colonists (settlers) come to this country? _____

_____

Put a line under the words in the passage that answer each question. If you are not sure, read it again and check your answers before you go on to the next section. At the end of this unit is a summary of steps called How to Move from Alien to Citizen. Read it as you did this reading exercise. Put lines under words that you do not understand. Later, look them up in the Word List.

See the answer key on page 181.

2. WHAT CITIZENSHIP MEANS

Do you know what a citizen is? A **citizen** is a part of his or her country. In the United States, a citizen is a free man or woman—free to make choices and free to help pick the people who govern. The opposite of a citizen is an **alien,** or stranger. You want to become a citizen! A person who likes the business he or she works for may want to become a partner, but it is not always easy to become a partner in a business. The United States government, however, makes it easy for you to become a partner in *its* business.

A citizen has many rights. The most important one is the right to vote. A citizen can vote in national, state, and local elections. A citizen helps to decide who will be president of the United States and who will make the laws for the nation, state, and city. A citizen can also vote for the local school board, the group of men and women who decide on the policies for the public schools.

There are other rights. For example, certain jobs are open only to citizens. These are often government jobs that offer security and many benefits. There is no question of a citizen's legal rights to receive Social Security payments in later life or to obtain welfare, if needed. American citizens with American passports are free to travel all over the world. Citizens do not have to report changes of address to the USCIS within 10 days of occurrence, as aliens must.

To sum up, a citizen belongs. But nothing in life comes free. There are costs to be shared. Yes, there is a price, but the price is right! You will learn what that price is.

Review

Do you know what these words mean? Write the meaning next to each word. If you are not sure, look up the meaning in the Word List in the Appendix.

1. alien _____

2. citizen _____

3. democracy_____

4. security _____

5. benefit_____

Now read the following questions. Write the answers in the spaces provided.

6. The opposite of *right* is *wrong.*

   a. What is the opposite of *citizen?* _____

   _____

   b. What is the opposite of *difficult?* _____

   _____

7. If you study all the lessons in this book, will it be easy or difficult to become

   a citizen?_____

   _____

8. Do you want to be a citizen or an alien? _____

   _____

9. What are some of the benefits of citizenship?_____

   _____

10. What are some of the rights of a citizen that you want to have? _____

   _____

See the answer key on page 181.

3. WHAT NATURALIZATION MEANS

Naturalization includes the word *natural* and it means giving an alien (or foreign-born person) the rights and privileges of a natural-born citizen.

   Naturalization means taking certain steps set by law to become a citizen. These steps are petitioning or asking for citizenship, proving eligibility and residence here, and taking the Oath of Allegiance (a promise of loyalty) to the United States of America.

   Look at the people you meet on the job, in your neighborhood, at school, and in government offices. Most of them are citizens. Some of them were born here;

others were **naturalized.** These others came here as strangers or immigrants and became citizens by naturalization.

Immigrants are people who enter the country for the purpose of living here. We are a nation of immigrants, as President John F. Kennedy told us in his book of that title. He said that the first settlers who came to this country in the 16th century and those who come today, wanting to live here, are all immigrants or the children of immigrants!

Another president, George H. W. Bush, said that America's greatness was "forged (created) by the talents, the hard work, and the hopes of people who came to our shores." He said that at a naturalization ceremony on Citizenship Day, September 17, 1988, before he became president.

"Welcome, new Americans," those are the words that open the naturalization ceremony. You will also hear those words when you are sworn in. You may also hear something like this: "Be proud of your roots, love the places where you have lived, and be proud of your success in attaining citizenship!"

Let us look at the last step in the naturalization process. You are in a large courtroom in front of a judge. Perhaps, as in a big city, there are many other people there, too. Some of your friends and relatives may be there, sitting on the benches behind you.

The clerk of the court says the words of the Oath of Allegiance. You repeat the words. In brief, they say that you will be loyal to the Constitution and laws of the United States of America. That is what you swear to do.

Other people who by law must take oaths like this one are the president and vice president, as well as many high government officials. The oath ends with the words, *So help me, God!*

After taking this oath, you are an American citizen. You will receive your Certificate of Naturalization (citizenship papers). Now, you have all the benefits of citizenship.

You are not an alien or stranger, but a part of this country! You can vote, run for office, and be elected to all positions except two: the president and vice president of the United States of America.

You have read about the last step in the naturalization process. In Part Two you will go back to the beginning and find out what the first step is. But first, do the review exercise that starts on this page. And read passages 4, 5, 6, and 7.

REVIEW

Do you know what these words mean? Write the meaning next to each word. If you are not sure, look up the meanings in the Word List in the Appendix.

1. naturalized _____

2. settle _____

3. immigrant _____

4. refugee _____

5. oath _____

  6. allegiance _____

  7. persecution _____

  8. political opinion _____

Now, write the answers to the following questions in the space provided.

  9. Where does naturalization take place?_____

_____

 10. What is the Oath of Allegiance?_____

_____

 11. Why do you want to become a citizen of the United States? _____

_____

 12. Can a naturalized citizen become a U.S. senator, a mayor, a governor? _____

_____

 13. Can a naturalized citizen become president of the United States (or vice

president)? _____

_____

See the answer key on page 182.

4. RIGHTS OF CITIZENS

The Constitution is the supreme, or highest, law of the United States. It was written in 1787 and became the law of the land for the United States of America in 1789. Since that time, it has been changed, or **amended,** 27 times. This means that there are 27 amendments to the Constitution of the United States of America. The Fourteenth Amendment was adopted in 1868 following the end of slavery in the United States. The amendment states the rights of citizens, as follows:

> **All persons born or naturalized in the United States, and subject to the <u>jurisdiction</u> thereof, are citizens of the United States and of the State <u>wherein they reside.</u> No state shall make or enforce any law which shall <u>abridge</u> the privileges or <u>immunities</u> of citizens of the United States; nor shall any State <u>deprive</u> any person of life, liberty, or property, without due process of law; nor deny to any person within its <u>jurisdiction</u> the equal protection of the laws.**

Here is the same article stated in simple English:

All persons born or naturalized in the United States, and living here under U.S. law, are citizens of the United States and of the state in which they live (reside). No state can make or carry out a law that limits (abridges) a citizen's Constitutional privileges or freedom. And no state can take away (deprive) life, liberty, or property without following fixed legal rules and procedures. All citizens are to be treated equally under the law and are entitled to the same protection within each state. Wherever a citizen travels, he or she is protected by the United States of America.

A citizen has a voice in the government. Only a citizen can vote for the officials who make the rules under which he or she lives, and only a citizen can hold office if elected. A citizen may work for the government under civil service.

REVIEW

Do you know what these words mean? Write the meanings next to the words. If you are not sure, look up the meaning in the Word List in the Appendix.

1. amendment _____

2. jurisdiction _____

3. residence_____

4. abridge _____

5. immunity_____

6. deprive _____

Now write the answers to the following questions in the space provided.

7. What is the highest law of the land? _____

_____

8. How many amendments are there?_____

_____

9. Which amendment tells about the rights of citizens? _____

_____

10. Can you tell what these rights are? _____

_____

Figure 2

Source: U.S. Department of Justice, Immigration and Naturalization Service

11. Which of the rights is the most important to you?_____

_____

See the answer key on page 182.

5. RESPONSIBILITIES OF CITIZENS

Citizenship has many benefits and all citizens must pay for these benefits; the price was right.

There is a Spanish proverb that tells us to "take what we want and pay for it." We have made a choice. We have chosen to become citizens. Now we must pay for that choice. We must register to vote and then vote on Election Day. We must work with others to make this a better place in which to live. Our government is a **democracy.** This means that through our vote we have a voice in government. We also have the right to join a political party. In doing so, we join with others who feel as we do.

Knowing all you can about the issues and keeping up-to-date on what is going on in your country are other responsibilities. The quality of government is improved when voters know who the candidates for office are.

When persons are tried for criminal or civil offenses, they are often judged guilty or innocent by a jury of their peers. This means that people who are citizens have to be willing to give their time to serve on a jury. When you become a citizen, you may be called for jury duty. One of the prices of citizenship is to be willing to serve if you are called. You will not be called more than once a year.

We can say that the price of citizenship includes doing the following:

- Keeping informed about what is going on
- Voting in every election
- Obeying the laws
- Paying taxes
- Defending the country if it becomes necessary *
- Serving on a jury if called
- Being willing to hold office

QUIZ

Do you know what these words mean? Write the meanings next to the words. If you are not sure, look them up in the Word List in the Appendix.

1. benefit_____

2. democracy_____

3. responsibility _____

4. informed _____

_____
*If it is not against your religion to do so.

5. criminal_____

6. civil_____

7. jury_____

Now write the answers to these questions in the space provided.

8. Are all the benefits of citizenship free?_____

_____

9. What is the price of citizenship?_____

_____

10. Why should a citizen vote?_____

_____

11. Why should a citizen serve on a jury?_____

_____

12. What are the responsibilities of citizenship?_____

_____

See the answer key on page 182.

6. EXCEPTIONS TO SOME REQUIREMENTS FOR NATURALIZATION

In reviewing the main requirements for naturalization (see pages xii–xiii), note that there are some *exceptions*. For example:

Item 3—You must have been a legal resident of the United States continuously for at least five years. Some exceptions to this rule are wives, husbands, or children of citizens, or persons in the armed forces or navy. See pages 177–180 for other exceptions.

Item 4—You must understand English and be able to read, write, and speak ordinary English. One exception to this rule is an applicant who is older than 50 years old and has lived in the United States as a permanent resident for at least 20 years. Another exception is an applicant who is older than 55 years old who has lived in the United States as a permanent resident for at least 15 years.

Item 5—You must have a knowledge and understanding of the history and government of the United States. An applicant who has a physical or developmental disability or a mental impairment may be eligible for an exception to this requirement. You must file Form N-648, Medical Certification for Disability Exceptions.

Item 6—You must be prepared to take the Oath of Allegiance to the United States. The USCIS may excuse some applicants from this requirement.

Answer the test that follows.

TEST

Answer these four questions. Check your answers with the answer key on page 182.

1. Item 1 of the requirements was left out in this passage. Do you remember

what it was? _____

2. Is there any exception to that requirement? _____

3. What is one exception to the residence requirement? _____

_____

4. Is there any exception to the requirement that you must take and

understand the Oath of Allegiance to the United States?_____

_____

You should also know the names of your two senators and the congressman or congresswoman who represents you.

Write them here: **SENATOR** _____

SENATOR _____

REPRESENTATIVE (MEMBER OF CONGRESS)

_____

You have read six (6) passages containing words connected with naturalization and citizenship, and you have taken short tests on your reading. Have you done well? Do you feel that you understand what you have read? Let us see about that!

Now read number 7, the summary. See if you can explain, in your own words, about moving from alien to citizen. Practice writing about it, too.

7. SUMMARY: HOW TO MOVE FROM ALIEN TO CITIZEN

Moving from alien to citizen is set by law. Immigration laws are made by the Congress of the United States. Everything in this book is in accord with the most recent Immigration and Nationality Act, and reflects all laws and regulations as of May 2013. A lawfully admitted alien can be naturalized if he or she meets the requirements (see pages xii–xiii and 177–180).

The law states that "a person may only be naturalized as a citizen of the United States in the manner and under the conditions prescribed, and not otherwise." In this unit you have read what these conditions are. You know that what is prescribed is what must be followed. You can do it, as many before you have done!

As one of our presidents wrote, our country is "a nation of immigrants." If the number of immigrants comes in at the current rate, we will continue this way. And some, like you, will aspire to citizenship. As you know, it takes time to become a full American citizen. Those who use their time wisely to prepare themselves will succeed.

This is the end of Part One.

PART TWO

APPLYING FOR U.S. CITIZENSHIP

An Introduction

First, read this brief review of the law:

The Immigration and Nationality Act requires you to have an understanding of the English language, history, principles, and form of government of the United States. You must be able to read, write, and speak words in ordinary usage in the English language, UNLESS you are older than 50 years old and have resided here for 20 years, or older than 55 years old and have resided here for 15 years, or have a physical or developmental disability or a mental impairment. You must have a knowledge of the history, principles, and government of the United States, no matter what your age. The only exception to this requirement is a physical or mental disability. No person may apply who is opposed to our government or law, or who favors totalitarian forms of government.

WHO CAN APPLY?

A lawfully admitted adult, at least 18 years of age, who has resided in the United States for five years or more as a permanent resident, or who has married a United States citizen and has lived with the spouse for three years or more.

All statements in this book are based on the Immigration and Nationality Act, and reflect regulations adopted as of May 11, 2013. See pages 177–180 for exceptions to the general requirements.

GETTING STARTED

Read this out loud:

I am eligible for naturalization because:

- I am 18 years old or older.
- I was legally admitted for permanent residence.
- I have resided here for at least five years, unless I have an exemption.
- I am a person of good moral character.
- I am willing to take the oath of allegiance to the United States of America.
- I meet the educational requirements, unless I have an exemption.

Did you understand all of that? Now read this:

This is Part Two. It contains five steps for you to follow to get ready for naturalization. They are:

Step 1: How to Begin
　　　　　　Forms and Fees
　　　　　　Some Questions You May Have
Step 2: Filing Your Form N-400
Step 3: Getting Fingerprinted
Step 4: Going to Your Interview
Step 5: Taking the Oath

Step 1—
How to Begin

FORMS AND FEES

Forms are available to use to apply for naturalization. These forms may be obtained from the USCIS webpage on the Internet at *http://uscis.gov*. You can also obtain these forms by calling the USCIS at 1-800-870-3676. Offices that help immigrants, such as attorneys or non-profit organizations, can also provide you with the correct forms to use.

> **WARNING:** People or websites may offer you USCIS forms if you pay a fee. These forms may be out of date or incorrect for your situation. Using them could slow down your application or cause serious legal problems. Current USCIS forms are available for free from the USCIS site, *http://uscis.gov*.
>
> People or websites may also offer you official-looking immigration cards for a fee. These are not real. Do not buy them. Only USCIS can give you an immigration document.

Before you obtain the forms and fill them out, it is important that you consult with an immigration attorney or a Board of Immigration Appeals (BIA) accredited representative. It is very important that you make sure you are eligible to apply for naturalization before you send in paperwork to the government. It is also very important that you consult with someone who knows immigration law and is authorized to help immigrants apply for naturalization and other immigration benefits. Many people, such as *notarios*, say they can help immigrants become a citizen, but they cannot. They take an immigrant's money, create problems for the immigrant, and sometimes, cause the immigrant to be deported. Be very careful who you ask to help you.

After you talk to an authorized legal service provider, then you can decide if you are eligible for naturalization and want to apply. You will need to provide several pieces of information, and you will need to pay a fee to USCIS.

This book includes a sample N-400 form for you to use to learn what information is needed to apply to become a citizen. Read the instructions carefully. As practice, fill out the form completely. Perhaps you are eligible to become a U.S. citizen!

FORM NUMBER	FORM TITLE	FORM FEE*
N-400	Application for Naturalization	$680
N-470	Application to Preserve Residence for Naturalization Purposes	$330
N-565	Application for Replacement of Naturalization/Citizenship Documents	$345
N-600	Application for Certificate of Citizenship	$600
N-600K	Application for Citizenship and Issuance of a Certificate Under Section 322	##
N-648	Medical Certification for Disability Exceptions	None
AR-11	Alien's Change of Address Card	None
I-90	Application to Replace Permanent Resident Card	$450
I-130	Petition for Alien Relative	$420
I-485	Application to Register Permanent Residence or Adjust Status	$1,070

$600 for an application filed on behalf of a biological child.
$550 for an application filed on behalf of an adopted child.

*As of May 13, 2013   Fees include the $85 biometrics fee for fingerprinting.

OMB No. 1615-0052; Expires 03/31/2013

Department of Homeland Security
U.S. Citizenship and Immigration Services

Instructions for Form N-400, Application for Naturalization

Instructions

Read these instructions carefully to properly complete this form. If you need more space to complete an answer, use a separate sheet of paper. Write your name and Alien Registration Number (USCIS A-Number), if any, at the top of each sheet of paper and indicate the part and number of the item to which the answer refers.

What Is the Purpose of This Form?

Form N-400 is an application for U.S. citizenship (naturalization). For more information about the naturalization process and eligibility requirements, read *A Guide to Naturalization* (Form M-476). If you do not already have a copy of the *Guide*, you can get a copy from:

1. USCIS Web site (**www.uscis.gov**);

2. USCIS toll-free forms line at **1-800-870-3676**; or

3. USCIS National Customer Service Center (NCSC) at **1-800-375-5283 (TTY:1-800-767-1833)**.

When Should I Use This Form?

You may apply for naturalization when you meet **all** the requirements to become a U.S. citizen. The section of the *Guide* called "Who is Eligible for Naturalization" and the Eligibility Worksheet found in the back of the *Guide* are tools to help you determine whether you are eligible to apply for naturalization. You should complete the worksheet before filling out Form N-400.

If you are applying based on five years as a lawful permanent resident or based on three years as a lawful permanent resident married to a U.S. citizen, you may apply for naturalization up to 90 days before you meet the "continuous residence" requirement. You must meet all other requirements at the time that you file your application with USCIS.

Certain applicants have different English and civics testing requirements based on their age and length of lawful permanent residence **at the time of filing**. If you are over 50 years of age and have lived in the United States as a lawful permanent resident for periods totaling at least 20 years, or if you are over 55 years of age and have lived in the United States as a lawful permanent resident for periods totaling at least 15 years, you do not have to take the English test, but you do have to take the civics test in the language of your choice.

If you are over 65 years of age and have lived in the United States as a lawful permanent resident for periods totaling at least 20 years, you do not have to take the English test, but you do have to take a simpler version of the civics test in the language of your choice.

Who May File This Form?

To use this form you must be **ONE** of the following:

1. A lawful permanent resident for at least five years and at least 18 years old; **or**

2. A lawful permanent resident for at least three years and at least 18 years old;

   AND

   You have been married to and living with the same U.S. citizen for the last three years;

   AND

   Your spouse has been a U.S. citizen for the last three years.

3. A member of one of several other groups eligible to apply for naturalization (for example, persons who are nationals but not citizens of the United States) and at least 18 years old. For more information about these groups, see the *Guide*.

4. A person who has served honorably in the U.S. Armed Forces;

   AND

   If you are at least 18 years old, a lawful permanent resident with at least one year of U.S. Armed Forces service, and you are filing your application for naturalization while still in the service or within six months after the termination of such service;

   OR

   You served honorably as a member of the Selected Reserve of the Ready Reserve or in active-duty status during a designated period of hostilities. You then may apply for naturalization without having been physically present in the United States for any specified period.

Figure 3

For more information, go to the USCIS Web site at **www.uscis.gov**.

NOTE: If you are married to a U.S. citizen who is employed or deployed abroad, in some circumstances you may be eligible for expedited naturalization under section 319(b) of the Immigration and Nationality Act (INA). For further assistance, see the *Guide*.

Who May Not File This Form?

In certain cases, a person who was born outside of the United States to U.S. citizen parents is already a citizen and does not need to apply for naturalization. To find out more information about this type of citizenship and whether you should file Form N-600, Application for Certificate of Citizenship, read the *Guide*.

Other permanent residents under 18 years of age may be eligible for U.S. citizenship if their U.S. citizen parent or parents file a Form N-600 application on their behalf. For more information, see "Frequently Asked Questions" in the *Guide*.

General Instructions

Step 1. Fill Out Form N-400

1. Type or print legibly in black ink.

2. If extra space is needed to complete any item, attach a continuation sheet, indicate the item number, and date and sign each sheet.

3. Answer all questions fully and accurately. State that an item is not applicable with "N/A." If the answer is none, write "None."

4. **Write your USCIS (or former INS) A-number on the top right hand corner of each page.** Use your A-number on your Permanent Resident Card (formerly known as the Alien Registration or "Green" Card). To locate your A-number, see the sample Permanent Resident Cards in the *Guide*. The A-number on your card consists of seven to nine numbers, depending on when your record was created. If the A-number on your card has fewer than nine numbers, place enough zeros before the first number to make a *total of nine numbers* on the application. For example, write card number A1234567 as A001234567, but write card number A12345678 as A012345678.

5. Answer all questions fully and accurately.

Step-by-Step Instructions

This form is divided into 14 parts. The information below will help you fill out the form.

Part 1. Your Name *(the person applying for naturalization)*

   A. **Your current legal name -** Your current legal name is the name on your birth certificate unless it has been changed after birth by a legal action such as a marriage or court order.

   B. **Your name exactly as it appears on your Permanent Resident Card** *(if different from above)* - Write your name exactly as it appears on your card, even if it is misspelled.

   C. **Other names you have used** - If you have used any other names, write them in this section. If you need more space, use a separate sheet of paper.

   If you have **never** used a different name, write "N/A" in the space for "Family Name *(Last Name)*."

   D. **Name change** *(optional)* - A court can allow a change in your name when you are being naturalized. A name change does not become final until a court naturalizes you. For more information regarding a name change, see the *Guide*.

   If you want a court to change your name at a naturalization oath ceremony, check "Yes" and complete this section. If you do not want to change your name, check "No" and go to Part 2.

Part 2. Information About Your Eligibility

Check the box that shows why you are eligible to apply for naturalization. If the basis for your eligibility is not described in one of the first three boxes, check "Other" and briefly write the basis for your application on the lines provided.

Part 3. Information About You

   A. **U.S. Social Security Number** - Print your U.S. Social Security Number. If you do not have one, write "N/A" in the space provided.

   B. **Date of birth** - Always use eight numbers to show your date of birth. Write the date in this order: Month, Day, Year. For example, write May 1, 1958, as 05/01/1958.

   C. **Date you became a permanent resident** - Write the official date when your lawful permanent residence began, as shown on your Permanent Resident Card. To help locate the date on your card, see the sample Permanent Resident Cards in the *Guide*. Write the date in this order: Month, Day, Year. For example, write August 9, 1988, as 08/09/1988.

   D. **Country of birth** - Write the name of the country where you were born. Write the name of the country even if it no longer exists.

Figure 3 (cont.)

E. **Country of Nationality** - Write the name of the country(ies) where you are currently a citizen or national.

   1. If you are stateless, write the name of the country where you were last a citizen or national.

   2. If you are a citizen or national of more than one country, write the name of the foreign country that issued your last passport.

F. **Citizenship of parents** - Check "Yes" if either of your parents is a U.S. citizen. If you answer "Yes," you may already be a citizen. For more information, see "Frequently Asked Questions" in the *Guide*.

G. **Current marital status** - Check the marital status you have on the date you are filing this application. If you are currently not married, but had a prior marriage that was annulled or otherwise legally terminated, check "Other" and explain it.

H. **Request for disability waiver** - If you have a medical disability or impairment that you believe qualifies you for a waiver of the tests of English and/or U.S. Government and history, check "Yes" and attach a properly completed Form N-648, Medical Certification for Disability Exceptions. If you ask for this waiver, it does not guarantee that you will be excused from the testing requirements. For more information about this waiver, see the *Guide*.

I. **Request for disability accommodations** - We will make every reasonable effort to help applicants with disabilities complete the naturalization process. For example, if you use a wheelchair, we will make sure that you can be fingerprinted and interviewed, and can attend a naturalization ceremony at a location that is wheelchair accessible. If you are deaf or hearing impaired and need a sign language interpreter, we will make arrangements with you to have one at your interview.

If you believe you will need us to modify or change the naturalization process for you, check the box or write in the space the kind of accommodation you need. If you need more space, use a separate sheet of paper. You do not need to send us Form N-648 to request an accommodation. You only need to send Form N-648 to request a waiver of the test of English and/or civics.

We consider requests for accommodations on a case-by-case basis. Asking for an accommodation will not affect your eligibility for citizenship.

Part 4. Information About Contacting You

A. **Home address** - Give the address where you now live. Do **not** put post office (P.O.) box numbers here.

B. **Mailing address** - If your mailing address is the same as your home address, write "Same." If your mailing address is different from your home address, write it in this part.

C. **Telephone numbers** - By giving us your telephone numbers and e-mail address, we can contact you about your application more quickly. If you are hearing impaired and use a TTY telephone connection, please indicate this by writing (TTY) after the telephone number.

Part 5. Information for Criminal Records Search

The Federal Bureau of Investigation (FBI) will use the information in this section, together with your fingerprints, to search for criminal records. Although the results of this search may affect your eligibility, we do **not** make naturalization decisions based on your gender, race, or physical description.

For each item, check the box or boxes that best describes you. The categories are those used by the FBI. You can select one or more.

NOTE: As part of the USCIS biometrics service requirement, you must be fingerprinted after you file this application. If necessary, USCIS may also take your photograph and signature.

Part 6. Information About Your Residence and Employment

A. Write every address where you have lived during the last five years (including in other countries).

Begin with where you live now. Include the dates you lived in those places. For example, write May 1998 to June 1999 as 05/1998 to 06/1999.

B. List where you have worked (or, if you were a student, the schools you have attended) during the last five years. Include military service. If you worked for yourself, write "Self employed." Begin with your most recent job. Also, write the dates when you worked or studied in each place.

If you need separate sheets of paper to complete section A or B or any other questions on this application, be sure to follow the instructions under **"Step 1. Fill Out Form N-400"** on **Page 2**.

Part 7. Time Outside the United States (*including trips to Canada, Mexico, and the Caribbean*)

A. Write the total number of days you spent outside of the United States (including military service) during the last five years. Count the days of every trip that lasted 24 hours or longer.

Figure 3 (cont.)

B. Write the number of trips you have taken outside the United States during the last five years. Count every trip that lasted 24 hours or longer.

C. Provide the requested information for every trip that you have taken outside the United States since you became a lawful permanent resident. Begin with your most recent trip.

Part 8. Information About Your Marital History

A. Write the number of times you have been married. Include any annulled marriages. If you were married to the same spouse more than one time, count each time as a separate marriage.

B. If you are now married, provide information about your current spouse.

C. Check the box to indicate whether your current spouse is a U.S. citizen.

D. If your spouse is a citizen through naturalization, give the date and place of naturalization. If your spouse regained U.S. citizenship, write the date and place the citizenship was regained.

E. If your spouse is not a U.S. citizen, complete this section.

F. If you were married before, give information about your former spouse or spouses. In question F.2, check the box showing the immigration status your former spouse had during your marriage. If the spouse was not a U.S. citizen or a lawful permanent resident at that time, check "Other" and explain. For question F.5, if your marriage was annulled, check "Other" and explain. If you were married to the same spouse more than one time, write about each marriage separately.

G. For any prior marriages of your current spouse, follow the instructions in section F above.

NOTE: If you or your present spouse had more than one prior marriage, provide the same information required by section F and section G about every additional marriage on a separate sheet of paper.

Part 9. Information About Your Children

A. Write the total number of sons and daughters you have had. Count **all** of your children, regardless of whether they are:

   1. Alive, missing, or dead;

   2. Born in other countries or in the United States;

   3. Under 18 years old or adults;

   4. Married or unmarried;

   5. Living with you or elsewhere;

   6. Stepsons or stepdaughters or legally adopted; or

   7. Born when you were not married.

B. Write information about all your sons and daughters. In the last column (Location), write:

   1. "With me" - if the son or daughter is currently living with you;

   2. The street address and state or country where the son or daughter lives - if the son or daughter is **not** currently living with you; or

   3. "Missing" or "Dead" - if that son or daughter is missing or dead.

NOTE: If you need space to list information about additional sons and daughters, attach a separate sheet of paper.

Part 10. Additional Questions

Answer each question by checking "Yes" or "No." If **any** part of a question applies to you, you must answer "Yes." For example, if you were never arrested but *were* once detained by a police officer, check "Yes" to the question "Have you ever been arrested or detained by a law enforcement officer?" and attach a written explanation.

We will use this information to determine your eligibility for citizenship. Answer every question honestly and accurately. If you do not, we may deny your application for lack of good moral character. Answering "Yes" to one of these questions does not always cause an application to be denied. For more information on eligibility, see the *Guide*.

Part 11. Your Signature

After reading the statement in Part 11, you must sign and date it. You should sign your full name without abbreviating it or using initials. The signature must be legible. Your application will be rejected if it is not signed.

If you cannot sign your name in English, sign in your native language. If you are unable to write in any language, sign your name with an "X."

NOTE: A designated representative may sign this section on behalf of an applicant who qualifies for a waiver of the Oath of Allegiance because of a developmental or physical impairment (see the *Guide* for more information). In such a case, the designated representative should write the name of the applicant and then sign his or her own name followed by the words "Designated Representative." The information attested to by the Designated Representative is subject to the same penalties discussed on **Page 8** of these instructions.

Part 12. Signature of Person Who Prepared this Application for You

If someone filled out this form for you, he or she must complete this section.

Figure 3 (cont.)

Part 13. Signature at Interview

Do not complete this part. You will be asked to complete this part at your interview.

Part 14. Oath of Allegiance

Do not complete this part. You will be asked to complete this part at your interview.

If we approve your application, you must take this Oath of Allegiance to become a citizen. In limited cases, you can take a modified oath. The oath requirement cannot be waived unless you are unable to understand its meaning because of a physical or developmental disability or mental impairment. For more information, see the *Guide*. Your signature on this form only indicates that you have no objections to taking the Oath of Allegiance. **It does not mean that you have taken the oath or that you are naturalized**. If USCIS approves your application for naturalization, you must attend an oath ceremony and take the Oath of Allegiance to the United States.

Step 2. General Requirements

Photographs. You **must** submit two identical passport-style color photographs of yourself taken within 30 days of the filing of this application. The photos must have a white to off-white background, be printed on thin paper with a glossy finish, and be unmounted and unretouched.

The photos must be 2" x 2" and must be in color with full face, frontal view on a white to off-white background. Head height should measure 1" to 1 3/8" from top of hair to bottom of chin, and eye height is between 1 1/8" to 1 3/8" from bottom of photo. Your head must be bare unless you are wearing a headdress as required by a religious order of which you are a member; however, your face must be visible. Using pencil or felt pen, lightly print your name and Alien Registration Number on the back of each photo.

NOTE: Any digital photo submitted needs to be produced from a high-resolution camera with at least 3.5 mega pixels of resolution.

Copy of Permanent Resident Card. Applicants who are lawful permanent residents of the United States must submit photocopies (front and back) of Form I-551 (Permanent Resident Card). If you have lost your Form I-551, attach a copy of any other entry document or a photocopy of a receipt showing that you have filed Form I-90, Application to Replace Permanent Resident Card.

Other Documents. Depending on the circumstances, some applicants must send certain documents with their application.

For example, if you have been arrested or convicted of a crime, you must send a certified copy of the arrest report, court disposition, sentencing, and any other relevant documents, including any countervailing evidence concerning the circumstances of your arrest or conviction that you would

like USCIS to consider. Note that unless a traffic incident was alcohol or drug related, you do not need to submit documentation for traffic fines and incidents that did not involve an actual arrest if the only penalty was a fine of less than $500 or points on your driver's license.

For more information on the documents you must send with your application, see the Document Checklist in the *Guide*.

Translations. Any document containing foreign language submitted to USCIS must be accompanied by a full English language translation which the translator has certified as complete and accurate, and by the translator's certification that he or she is competent to translate from the foreign language into English.

Copies. Unless specifically required that an original document be filed with an application or petition, an ordinary legible photocopy may be submitted. Original documents submitted when not required will remain a part of the record, even if the submission was not required.

Where To File?

Mail your completed Form N-400 and accompanying documentation to the appropriate Lockbox facility.

If you reside in Alaska, Arizona, California, Colorado, Hawaii, Idaho, Illinois, Indiana, Iowa, Kansas, Michigan, Minnesota, Missouri, Montana, Nebraska, Nevada, North Dakota, Ohio, Oregon, South Dakota, Utah, Washington, Wisconsin, Wyoming, Territory of Guam, or the Commonwealth of the Northern Mariana Islands, send your Form N-400 to the **USCIS Phoenix Lockbox** facility at the following address:

> **USCIS**
> **P.O. Box 21251**
> **Phoenix, AZ 85036**

For Express Mail or commercial courier deliveries, use the following address:

> **USCIS**
> **Attn: N-400**
> **1820 E. Skyharbor Circle S Ste 100**
> **Phoenix, AZ 85034**

If you reside in Alabama, Arkansas, Connecticut, Delaware, District of Columbia, Florida, Georgia, Kentucky, Louisiana, Maine, Maryland, Massachusetts, Mississippi, New Hampshire, New Jersey, New Mexico, New York, North Carolina, Oklahoma, Pennsylvania, Rhode Island, South Carolina, Tennessee, Texas, Vermont, Virginia, West Virginia, Commonwealth of Puerto Rico, or the U.S. Virgin Islands, send your Form N-400 to the **USCIS Dallas Lockbox** facility at the following address:

Figure 3 (cont.)

USCIS
P.O. 660060
Dallas, TX 75266

For Express Mail or commercial courier deliveries, use the following address:

USCIS
Attn: N-400
2501 S. State Hwy 121 Business Ste 400
Lewisville, TX 75067

Current or former members of the U.S. Armed Forces, spouses of current members of the U.S. Armed Forces, or close relatives of deceased members of the U.S. Armed Forces.

You must send all Form N-400 applications filed under the military provisions, sections 328 or 329 of the INA, to the **USCIS Nebraska Service Center** at the address below regardless of where you live and whether you are filing from within the United States or abroad.

Also, if you are the spouse of a current member of the U.S. Armed Forces, or are the close relative of a member of the U.S. Armed Forces (see section 319(d) of the INA), send your Form N-400 to the **USCIS Nebraska Service Center** at the address below regardless of where you live and whether you are filing from within the United States or abroad.

USCIS Nebraska Service Center
P.O. Box 87426
Lincoln, NE 68501-7426

For Express Mail or commercial courier deliveries, use the following address:

USCIS Nebraska Service Center
850 S Street
Lincoln, NE 68508

Section 319(b) of the INA Applicants

If you are filing under section 319(b) of the INA because you are the spouse of a U.S. citizen who is employed abroad, and the U.S. citizen spouse's employment meets the criteria for naturalization under section 319(b) of the INA, you must send your Form N-400 to the **USCIS Phoenix Lockbox** facility regardless of where you live and whether you are filing from within the United States or abroad. **However, if you are filing under 319(b) and are a spouse of a current member of the U.S. Armed Forces, file with the USCIS Nebraska Service Center as instructed above.**

USCIS
Attn: N-400
P.O. Box 21251
Phoenix, AZ 85036

For Express Mail or commercial courier deliveries, use the following address:

USCIS
Attn: N-400 319(b)
1820 E. Skyharbor Circle S Ste 100
Phoenix, AZ 85034

E-Notification

If you are filing your Form N-400 at one of the USCIS Lockbox facilities, you may elect to receive an e-mail and/or text message notifying you that your application has been accepted. You must complete Form G-1145, E-Notification of Application/Petition Acceptance, and clip it to the first page of your application. To download a copy of Form G-1145, including the instructions, visit the USCIS Web site at www.uscis.gov/G-1145.

For further information on where to file, including if you are currently overseas, read the section in the *Guide* titled "Completing Your Application and Getting Photographed" or call the NCSC at 1-800-375-5283 (TTY: 1-800-767-1833) or visit our Web site at www.uscis.gov and click on "**FORMS**."

What Is the Filing Fee?

The filing fee for Form N-400 is **$595.**

An additional biometrics services fee of **$85** is required when filing Form N-400. After you submit Form N-400, USCIS will notify you about when and where to go for biometrics services.

Applicants 75 years of age or older are exempt from the biometrics services fee. Individuals who require fingerprinting and who reside outside of the United States at the time of filing an application or petition for immigration benefits are exempt from biometrics services fee.

NOTE: All naturalization applicants filing under the military provisions, section 328 or 329 of the INA, do not require a filing fee.

You may submit one check or money order for both the application and biometrics services fees, for a total of **$680.**

Use the following guidelines when you prepare your check or money order for Form N-400 and the biometrics services fees:

1. The check or money order must be drawn on a bank or other financial institution located in the United States and must be payable in U.S. currency; **and**

2. Make the check or money order payable to **U.S. Department of Homeland Security**.

   NOTE: Spell out U.S. Department of Homeland Security; do not use the initials "USDHS" or "DHS."

Figure 3 (cont.)

Notice to Those Making Payment by Check. If you send us a check, it will be converted into an electronic funds transfer (EFT). This means we will copy your check and use the account information on it to electronically debit your account for the amount of the check. The debit from your account will usually take 24 hours and will be shown on your regular account statement.

You will not receive your original check back. We will destroy your original check, but we will keep a copy of it. If the EFT cannot be processed for technical reasons, you authorize us to process the copy in place of your original check. If the EFT cannot be completed because of insufficient funds, we may try to make the transfer up to two times.

How to Check If the Fees Are Correct

The form and biometrics services fees on this form are current as of the edition date appearing in the lower right corner of this page. However, because USCIS fees change periodically, you can verify if the fees are correct by following one of the steps below:

1. Visit the USCIS Web site at <u>www.uscis.gov</u>, select "**FORMS**," and check the appropriate fee;

2. Review the Fee Schedule included in your form package, if you called us to request the form; or

3. Telephone the USCIS National Customer Service Center at **1-800-375-5283** and ask for the fee information.

NOTE: If your Form N-400 requires payment of a biometrics services fee for USCIS to take your fingerprints, photograph, or signature, you can use the same procedure to obtain the correct biometrics services fee.

Processing Information

Any Form N-400 that is not signed or accompanied by the correct fee will be rejected. Any application that is not completed in accordance with these instructions, is missing pages or otherwise not executed in its entirety, or is not accompanied by the required initial evidence may also be rejected. If your Form N-400 is rejected, the form and any fees will be returned to you and you will be notified why the form is considered deficient. You may correct the deficiency and resubmit Form N-400. An application or petition is not considered properly filed until accepted by USCIS.

Requests for more information or interview. USCIS may request more information or evidence, or request that you appear at a USCIS office for an interview. USCIS may also request that you submit the originals of any copy. USCIS will return these originals when they are no longer required.

Decision. The decision on Form N-400 involves a determination of whether you have established eligibility for the requested benefit. If you do not establish a basis for eligibility, USCIS will deny your Form N-400. You will be notified of the decision in writing.

Address Changes

If you have changed your address, you must inform USCIS of your new address. For information on filing a change of address go to the USCIS Web site at <u>www.uscis.gov/addresschange</u> or contact the USCIS National Customer Service Center at **1-800-375-5283**.

NOTE: Do not submit a change of address request to the USCIS Lockbox facilities because the Lockbox facilities do not process change of address requests.

Current Members of the U.S. Armed Forces

Contact the Military Help Line at **1-877-247-4645** if you are transferred to a new duty station after you file your Form N-400. **This includes deploying overseas or on a vessel.**

USCIS Forms and Information

You can get USCIS forms and immigration-related information on the USCIS Web site at <u>www.uscis.gov</u>. You may order USCIS forms by calling our toll-free number at **1-800-870-3676**. You may also obtain forms and information by telephoning the USCIS National Customer Service Center at **1-800-375-5283**.

As an alternative to waiting in line for assistance at your local USCIS office, you can now schedule an appointment through our Internet-based system, **InfoPass**. To access the system, visit our Web site. Use the **InfoPass** appointment scheduler and follow the screen prompts to set up your appointment. **InfoPass** generates an electronic appointment notice that appears on the screen.

NOTE: Schedule an InfoPass appointment if you do not know your USCIS A-Number or permanent resident date to obtain this information **BEFORE** you file your Form N-400.

Penalties

If you knowingly and willfully falsify or conceal a material fact or submit a false document with this Form N-400, we will deny your Form N-400 and may deny any other immigration benefit.

In addition, you will face severe penalties provided by law and may be subject to criminal prosecution.

Figure 3 (cont.)

USCIS Privacy Act Statement

AUTHORITIES: The information requested on this form request, and the associated evidence, is collected under the Immigration and Nationality Act, section 101, et seq.

PURPOSE: The primary purpose for providing the requested information on this form is to determine if you have established eligibility for the immigration benefit for which you are filing. The information you provide will be used to grant or deny the benefit sought.

DISCLOSURE: The information you provide is voluntary. However, failure to provide the requested information, and any requested evidence, may delay a final decision or result in denial of your form.

ROUTINE USES: The information you provide on this form may be shared with other Federal, State, local, and foreign government agencies and authorized organizations following approved routine uses described in the associated published system of records notices [DHS-USCIS-007 - Benefits Information System and DHS-USCIS-001 - Alien File (A-File) and Central Index System (CIS), which can be found at **www.dhs.gov/privacy**]. The information may also be made available, as appropriate, for law enforcement purposes or in the interest of national security.

Paperwork Reduction Act

An agency may not conduct or sponsor an information collection, and a person is not required to respond to a collection of information unless it displays a currently valid OMB control number. The public reporting burden for this collection of information is estimated at 6 hours and 8 minutes per response, including the time for reviewing instructions, and completing and submitting the form. Send comments regarding this burden estimate or any other aspect of this collection of information, including suggestions for reducing this burden, to: U.S. Citizenship and Immigration Services, Regulatory Products Division, Office of the Executive Secretariat, 20 Massachusetts Avenue, N.W., Washington, DC 20529-2020. OMB No. 1615-0052. **Do not mail your completed N-400 application to this address.**

Figure 3 (cont.)

Fill out this form in **pencil** for practice.

OMB No. 1615-0052; Expires 03/31/2013

**N-400 Application
for Naturalization**

Department of Homeland Security
U.S Citizenship and Immigration Services

Print clearly or type your answers using CAPITAL letters. Failure to print clearly may delay your application. Use black ink.

Part 1. Your Name (*Person applying for naturalization*)	Write your USCIS A-Number here:
	A

A. Your current legal name.

Family Name (*Last Name*)

Given Name (*First Name*)   Full Middle Name (*If applicable*)

B. Your name **exactly** as it appears on your Permanent Resident Card.

Family Name (*Last Name*)

Given Name (*First Name*)   Full Middle Name (*If applicable*)

C. If you have ever used other names, provide them below.

Family Name (*Last Name*)	Given Name (*First Name*)	Middle Name

D. Name change (*optional*)

Read the Instructions before you decide whether to change your name.

1. Would you like to legally change your name?   ☐ Yes   ☐ No

2. If "Yes," print the new name you would like to use. Do not use initials or
abbreviations when writing your new name.

Family Name (*Last Name*)

Given Name (*First Name*)   Full Middle Name

For USCIS Use Only

Bar Code	Date Stamp

Remarks

Action Block

Part 2. Information About Your Eligibility (*Check only one*)

I am at least 18 years old **AND**

A. ☐ I have been a lawful permanent resident of the United States for at least five years.

B. ☐ I have been a lawful permanent resident of the United States for at least three years, **and** I
have been married to and living with the same U.S. citizen for the last three years, **and** my
spouse has been a U.S. citizen for the last three years.

C. ☐ I am applying on the basis of qualifying military service.

D. ☐ Other (*Explain*) _____

Form N-400 (Rev. 03/22/12) Y

Figure 4

Part 3. Information About You	Write your USCIS A-Number here: A

A. U.S. Social Security Number   **B.** Date of Birth *(mm/dd/yyyy)*   **C.** Date You Became a Permanent Resident *(mm/dd/yyyy)*

D. Country of Birth   **E.** Country of Nationality

F. Are either of your parents U.S. citizens? *(If yes, see instructions)*   ☐ Yes   ☐ No

G. What is your current marital status?   ☐ Single, Never Married   ☐ Married   ☐ Divorced   ☐ Widowed

☐ Marriage Annulled or Other *(Explain)* _____

H. Are you requesting a waiver of the English and/or U.S. History and Government requirements based on a disability or impairment and attaching Form N-648 with your application?   ☐ Yes   ☐ No

I. Are you requesting an accommodation to the naturalization process because of a disability or impairment? *(See instructions for some examples of accommodations.)*   ☐ Yes   ☐ No

If you answered "Yes," check the box below that applies:

☐ I am deaf or hearing impaired and need a sign language interpreter who uses the following language: _____

☐ I use a wheelchair.

☐ I am blind or sight impaired.

☐ I will need another type of accommodation. Explain: _____

Part 4. Addresses and Telephone Numbers

A. Home Address - Street Number and Name *(Do **not** write a P.O. Box in this space.)*   Apartment Number

City	County	State	ZIP Code	Country

B. Care of   Mailing Address - Street Number and Name *(If different from home address)*   Apartment Number

City	State	ZIP Code	Country

C. Daytime Phone Number *(If any)*   Evening Phone Number *(If any)*   E-Mail Address *(If any)*

( )   ( )

Figure 4 (cont.)

Part 5. Information for Criminal Records Search

Write your USCIS A-Number here:
A

NOTE: The categories below are those required by the FBI. See instructions for more information.

A. Gender

☐ Male   ☐ Female

B. Height

Feet	Inches

C. Weight

Pounds

D. Are you Hispanic or Latino?   ☐ Yes   ☐ No

E. Race *(Select one or more)*

☐ White   ☐ Asian   ☐ Black or African American   ☐ American Indian or Alaskan Native   ☐ Native Hawaiian or Other Pacific Islander

F. Hair color

☐ Black   ☐ Brown   ☐ Blonde   ☐ Gray   ☐ White   ☐ Red   ☐ Sandy   ☐ Bald (No Hair)

G. Eye color

☐ Brown   ☐ Blue   ☐ Green   ☐ Hazel   ☐ Gray   ☐ Black   ☐ Pink   ☐ Maroon   ☐ Other

Part 6. Information About Your Residence and Employment

A. Where have you lived during the last five years? Begin with where you live now and then list every place you lived for the last five years. If you need more space, use a separate sheet of paper.

Street Number and Name, Apartment Number, City, State, Zip Code, and Country	Dates *(mm/dd/yyyy)*	
	From	To
Current Home Address - Same as Part 4.A		Present

B. Where have you worked (or, if you were a student, what schools did you attend) during the last five years? Include military service. Begin with your current or latest employer and then list every place you have worked or studied for the last five years. If you need more space, use a separate sheet of paper.

Employer or School Name	Employer or School Address *(Street, City, and State)*	Dates *(mm/dd/yyyy)*		Your Occupation
		From	To	

Figure 4 (cont.)

Part 7. Time Outside the United States
(Including Trips to Canada, Mexico and the Caribbean Islands)

Write your USCIS A-Number here:
A ·

A. How many total days did you spend outside of the United States during the past five years? ☐ days

B. How many trips of 24 hours or more have you taken outside of the United States during the past five years? ☐ trips

C. List below all the trips of 24 hours or more that you have taken outside of the United States since becoming a lawful permanent resident. Begin with your most recent trip. If you need more space, use a separate sheet of paper.

Date You Left the United States *(mm/dd/yyyy)*	Date You Returned to the United States *(mm/dd/yyyy)*	Did Trip Last Six Months or More?	Countries to Which You Traveled	Total Days Out of the United States
		☐ Yes ☐ No		
		☐ Yes ☐ No		
		☐ Yes ☐ No		
		☐ Yes ☐ No		
		☐ Yes ☐ No		
		☐ Yes ☐ No		
		☐ Yes ☐ No		
		☐ Yes ☐ No		
		☐ Yes ☐ No		
		☐ Yes ☐ No		

Part 8. Information About Your Marital History

A. How many times have you been married (including annulled marriages)? ☐ If you have **never** been married, go to Part 9.

B. If you are now married, give the following information about your spouse:

1. Spouse's Family Name *(Last Name)*   Given Name *(First Name)*   Full Middle Name *(If applicable)*

2. Date of Birth *(mm/dd/yyyy)*   **3.** Date of Marriage *(mm/dd/yyyy)*   **4.** Spouse's U.S. Social Security #

5. Home Address - Street Number and Name   Apartment Number

City   State   Zip Code

Figure 4 (cont.)

Part 8. Information About Your Marital History *(Continued)*

Write your USCIS A-Number here:
A

C. Is your spouse a U.S. citizen?   ☐ Yes   ☐ No

D. If your spouse is a U.S. citizen, give the following information:

    1. When did your spouse become a U.S. citizen?   ☐ At Birth   ☐ Other

    If "Other," give the following information:

    2. Date your spouse became a U.S. citizen

    3. Place your spouse became a U.S. citizen (*See instructions*)

    City and State

E. If your spouse is **not** a U.S. citizen, give the following information :

    1. Spouse's Country of Citizenship

    2. Spouse's USCIS A- Number (*If applicable*)

    A

    3. Spouse's Immigration Status

    ☐ Lawful Permanent Resident   ☐ Other _____

F. If you were married before, provide the following information about your prior spouse. If you have more than one previous marriage, use a separate sheet of paper to provide the information requested in Questions 1-5 below.

    1. Prior Spouse's Family Name (*Last Name*)   Given Name (*First Name*)   Full Middle Name (*If applicable*)

    2. Prior Spouse's Immigration Status

    ☐ U.S. Citizen
    ☐ Lawful Permanent Resident
    ☐ Other _____

    3. Date of Marriage (*mm/dd/yyyy*)

    4. Date Marriage Ended (*mm/dd/yyyy*)

    5. How Marriage Ended

    ☐ Divorce   ☐ Spouse Died   ☐ Other _____

G. How many times has your current spouse been married (including annulled marriages)?

    If your spouse has **ever** been married before, give the following information about **your spouse's** prior marriage.
    If your spouse has more than one previous marriage, use a separate sheet(s) of paper to provide the information requested in Questions 1 - 5 below.

    1. Prior Spouse's Family Name (*Last Name*)   Given Name (*First Name*)   Full Middle Name (*If applicable*)

    2. Prior Spouse's Immigration Status

    ☐ U.S. Citizen
    ☐ Lawful Permanent Resident
    ☐ Other _____

    3. Date of Marriage (*mm/dd/yyyy*)

    4. Date Marriage Ended (*mm/dd/yyyy*)

    5. How Marriage Ended

    ☐ Divorce   ☐ Spouse Died   ☐ Other _____

Figure 4 (cont.)

Part 9. Information About Your Children	Write your USCIS A-Number here: A

A. How many sons and daughters have you had? For more information on which sons and daughters you should include and how to complete this section, see the Instructions.

B. Provide the following information about all of your sons and daughters. If you need more space, use a separate sheet of paper.

Full Name of Son or Daughter	Date of Birth (mm/dd/yyyy)	USCIS A- number (if child has one)	Country of Birth	Current Address (Street, City, State and Country)
		A		
		A		
		A		
		A		
		A		
		A		
		A		
		A		

| Add Children | | | | Go to continuation page |

Part 10. Additional Questions

Answer Questions 1 through 14. If you answer "Yes" to any of these questions, include a written explanation with this form. Your written explanation should (1) explain why your answer was "Yes" and (2) provide any additional information that helps to explain your answer.

A. General Questions.

1. Have you **ever** claimed to be a U.S. citizen *(in writing or any other way)*? ☐ Yes ☐ No

2. Have you **ever** registered to vote in any Federal, State, or local election in the United States? ☐ Yes ☐ No

3. Have you **ever** voted in any Federal, State, or local election in the United States? ☐ Yes ☐ No

4. Since becoming a lawful permanent resident, have you **ever** failed to file a required Federal, State, or local tax return? ☐ Yes ☐ No

5. Do you owe any Federal, State, or local taxes that are overdue? ☐ Yes ☐ No

6. Do you have any title of nobility in any foreign country? ☐ Yes ☐ No

7. Have you ever been declared legally incompetent or been confined to a mental institution within the last five years? ☐ Yes ☐ No

Form N-400 (Rev. 03/22/12) Y Page 6

Figure 4 (cont.)

Part 10. Additional Questions *(Continued)*	Write your USCIS A-Number here: A

B. Affiliations.

8. **a**   Have you **ever** been a member of or associated with any organization, association, fund
foundation, party, club, society, or similar group in the United States or in any other place?   ☐ Yes   ☐ No

   b. If you answered "Yes," list the name of each group below. If you need more space, attach the names of the other group(s) on a
   separate sheet of paper.

Name of Group	Name of Group
1.	6.
2.	7.
3.	8.
4.	9.
5.	10.

9.   Have you **ever** been a member of or in any way associated *(either directly or indirectly)* with:

   a. The Communist Party?   ☐ Yes   ☐ No

   b. Any other totalitarian party?   ☐ Yes   ☐ No

   c. A terrorist organization?   ☐ Yes   ☐ No

10. Have you **ever** advocated *(either directly or indirectly)* the overthrow of any government
by force or violence?   ☐ Yes   ☐ No

11. Have you **ever** persecuted *(either directly or indirectly)* any person because of race,
religion, national origin, membership in a particular social group, or political opinion?   ☐ Yes   ☐ No

12. Between March 23, 1933, and May 8, 1945, did you work for or associate in any way *(either
directly or indirectly)* with:

   a. The Nazi government of Germany?   ☐ Yes   ☐ No

   b. Any government in any area (1) occupied by, (2) allied with, or (3) established with the
   help of the Nazi government of Germany?   ☐ Yes   ☐ No

   c. Any German, Nazi, or S.S. military unit, paramilitary unit, self-defense unit, vigilante unit,
   citizen unit, police unit, government agency or office, extermination camp, concentration
   camp, prisoner of war camp, prison, labor camp, or transit camp?   ☐ Yes   ☐ No

C. Continuous Residence.

Since becoming a lawful permanent resident of the United States:

13. Have you **ever** called yourself a "nonresident" on a Federal, State, or local tax return?   ☐ Yes   ☐ No

14. Have you **ever** failed to file a Federal, State, or local tax return because you considered
yourself to be a "nonresident"?   ☐ Yes   ☐ No

Figure 4 (cont.)

Part 10. Additional Questions *(continued)*	Write your USCIS A-Number here: A

D. Good Moral Character.

For the purposes of this application, you must answer "Yes" to the following questions, if applicable, even if your records were sealed or otherwise cleared or if anyone, including a judge, law enforcement officer, or attorney, told you that you no longer have a record.

15. Have you **ever** committed a crime or offense for which you were **not** arrested? ☐ Yes ☐ No

16. Have you **ever** been arrested, cited, or detained by any law enforcement officer (including USCIS or former INS and military officers) for any reason? ☐ Yes ☐ No

17. Have you **ever** been charged with committing any crime or offense? ☐ Yes ☐ No

18. Have you **ever** been convicted of a crime or offense? ☐ Yes ☐ No

19. Have you **ever** been placed in an alternative sentencing or a rehabilitative program (for example: diversion, deferred prosecution, withheld adjudication, deferred adjudication)? ☐ Yes ☐ No

20. Have you **ever** received a suspended sentence, been placed on probation, or been paroled? ☐ Yes ☐ No

21. Have you **ever** been in jail or prison? ☐ Yes ☐ No

If you answered "Yes" to any of Questions 15 through 21, complete the following table. If you need more space, use a separate sheet of paper to give the same information.

Why were you arrested, cited, detained, or charged?	Date arrested, cited, detained, or charged? *(mm/dd/yyyy)*	Where were you arrested, cited, detained, or charged? *(City, State, Country)*	Outcome or disposition of the arrest, citation, detention, or charge *(No charges filed, charges dismissed, jail, probation, etc.)*

Answer Questions 22 through 33. If you answer "Yes" to any of these questions, attach (1) your written explanation why your answer was "Yes" and (2) any additional information or documentation that helps explain your answer.

22. Have you **ever**:

    a. Been a habitual drunkard? ☐ Yes ☐ No

    b. Been a prostitute, or procured anyone for prostitution? ☐ Yes ☐ No

    c. Sold or smuggled controlled substances, illegal drugs, or narcotics? ☐ Yes ☐ No

    d. Been married to more than one person at the same time? ☐ Yes ☐ No

    e. Helped anyone enter or try to enter the United States illegally? ☐ Yes ☐ No

    f. Gambled illegally or received income from illegal gambling? ☐ Yes ☐ No

    g. Failed to support your dependents or to pay alimony? ☐ Yes ☐ No

23. Have you **ever** given false or misleading information to any U.S. Government official while applying for any immigration benefit or to prevent deportation, exclusion, or removal? ☐ Yes ☐ No

24. Have you **ever** lied to any U.S. Government official to gain entry or admission into the United States? ☐ Yes ☐ No

Figure 4 (cont.)

Part 10. Additional Questions *(Continued)*

Write your USCIS A-Number here:
A

E. Removal, Exclusion, and Deportation Proceedings.

25. Are removal, exclusion, rescission, or deportation proceedings pending against you?   ☐ Yes ☐ No

26. Have you **ever** been removed, excluded, or deported from the United States?   ☐ Yes ☐ No

27. Have you **ever** been ordered to be removed, excluded, or deported from the United States?   ☐ Yes ☐ No

28. Have you **ever** applied for any kind of relief from removal, exclusion, or deportation?   ☐ Yes ☐ No

F. Military Service.

29. Have you **ever** served in the U.S. Armed Forces?   ☐ Yes ☐ No

30. Have you **ever** left the United States to avoid being drafted into the U.S. Armed Forces?   ☐ Yes ☐ No

31. Have you **ever** applied for any kind of exemption from military service in the U.S. Armed Forces?   ☐ Yes ☐ No

32. Have you **ever** deserted from the U.S. Armed Forces?   ☐ Yes ☐ No

G. Selective Service Registration.

33. Are you a male who lived in the United States at any time between your 18th and 26th birthdays in any status except as a lawful nonimmigrant?   ☐ Yes ☐ No

    If you answered "NO," go on to question 34.

    If you answered "YES," provide the information below.

    If you answered "YES," but you did not register with the Selective Service System and are still under 26 years of age, you must register before you apply for naturalization, so that you can complete the information below:

    Date Registered (mm/dd/yyyy) [   ]   Selective Service Number [   ]

    If you answered "YES," but you did not register with the Selective Service and you are now 26 years old or older, attach a statement explaining why you did not register.

H. Oath Requirements. *(See Part 14 for the text of the oath)*

Answer Questions 34 through 39. If you answer "No" to any of these questions, attach (1) your written explanation why the answer was "No" and (2) any additional information or documentation that helps to explain your answer.

34. Do you support the Constitution and form of government of the United States?   ☐ Yes ☐ No

35. Do you understand the full Oath of Allegiance to the United States?   ☐ Yes ☐ No

36. Are you willing to take the full Oath of Allegiance to the United States?   ☐ Yes ☐ No

37. If the law requires it, are you willing to bear arms on behalf of the United States?   ☐ Yes ☐ No

38. If the law requires it, are you willing to perform noncombatant services in the U.S. Armed Forces?   ☐ Yes ☐ No

39. If the law requires it, are you willing to perform work of national importance under civilian direction?   ☐ Yes ☐ No

Form N-400 (Rev. 03/22/12) Y Page 9

Figure 4 (cont.)

Part 11. Your Signature

Write your USCIS A-Number here:
A

I certify, under penalty of perjury under the laws of the United States of America, that this application, and the evidence submitted with it, are all true and correct. I authorize the release of any information that the USCIS needs to determine my eligibility for naturalization.

Your Signature

Date *(mm/dd/yyyy)*

Part 12. Signature of Person Who Prepared This Application for You *(If applicable)*

I declare under penalty of perjury that I prepared this application at the request of the above person. The answers provided are based on information of which I have personal knowledge and/or were provided to me by the above named person in response to the *exact questions* contained on this form.

Preparer's Printed Name

Preparer's Signature

Date *(mm/dd/yyyy)*

Preparer's Firm or Organization Name *(If applicable)*

Preparer's Daytime Phone Number

Preparer's Address - Street Number and Name

City

State

Zip Code

NOTE: Do not complete Parts 13 and 14 until a USCIS Officer instructs you to do so.

Part 13. Signature at Interview

I swear (affirm) and certify under penalty of perjury under the laws of the United States of America that I know that the contents of this application for naturalization subscribed by me, including corrections numbered 1 through _____ and the evidence submitted by me numbered pages 1 through _____ , are true and correct to the best of my knowledge and belief.

Subscribed to and sworn to (affirmed) before me

Officer's Printed Name or Stamp

Date *(mm/dd/yyyy)*

Complete Signature of Applicant

Officer's Signature

Part 14. Oath of Allegiance

If your application is approved, you will be scheduled for a public oath ceremony at which time you will be required to take the following Oath of Allegiance immediately prior to becoming a naturalized citizen. By signing, you acknowledge your willingness and ability to take this oath:

I hereby declare, on oath, that I absolutely and entirely renounce and abjure all allegiance and fidelity to any foreign prince, potentate, state, or sovereignty, of whom or which I have heretofore been a subject or citizen;

that I will support and defend the Constitution and laws of the United States of America against all enemies, foreign and domestic;

that I will bear true faith and allegiance to the same;

that I will bear arms on behalf of the United States when required by the law;

that I will perform noncombatant service in the Armed Forces of the United States when required by the law;

that I will perform work of national importance under civilian direction when required by the law; and

that I take this obligation freely, without any mental reservation or purpose of evasion, so help me God.

Printed Name of Applicant

Complete Signature of Applicant

Form N-400 (Rev. 03/22/12) Y Page 10

Figure 4 (cont.)

Step 2— Filing Your Form N-400

How you fill out each form is very important. Forms must be typed or printed by hand in capital letters in black ink. Care must be taken that even the last copy can be read. All necessary documents should be included. Send copies of the documents unless the USCIS asks for the originals.

First, take out your Permanent Resident Card (green card). Your name, exactly as it is on the card, must be printed in Part 1. Be careful as you fill in your alien registration number and your Social Security number. If you are using a *different name* now, or if you used any other name in the past, that also goes in Part 1.

When you have completed your final form, you should mail it, with payment, to the appropriate regional office listed below. You may send it 90 days before you have the full residence time needed for your application. Include a check or money order for $680 made out to U.S. Department of Homeland Security. ($595 is the application fee, and $85 is the fingerprinting fee.) Also send in a copy of both sides of your Permanent Resident Card and two recent passport-size color photographs. The photographs should have your "A-number" written on the back. The pictures should be taken no more than 30 days earlier than the date you mailed your application to USCIS. Make copies of your N-400. Keep your copies in a safe place. Now mail "the real thing" and wait. You will hear from the USCIS telling you where and when to go to be fingerprinted.

Here is the list of regional offices:

If you live in Alabama, Arkansas, Connecticut, Delaware, District of Columbia, Florida, Georgia, Kentucky, Louisiana, Maine, Maryland, Massachusetts, Mississippi, New Hampshire, New Jersey, New Mexico, New York, North Carolina, Oklahoma, Pennsylvania, Puerto Rico, Rhode Island, South Carolina, Tennessee, Texas, Vermont, Virginia, West Virginia or U.S. Virgin Islands, send your application to:

USCIS Lockbox Facility
USCIS
P.O. Box 660060
Dallas, TX 75266

If you live in Alaska, Arizona, California, Colorado, Hawaii, Idaho, Illinois, Indiana, Iowa, Kansas, Michigan, Minnesota, Missouri, Montana, Nebraska, Nevada, North Dakota, Ohio, Oregon, South Dakota, Utah, Washington, Wisconsin, Wyoming, Territory of Guam, or Northern Mariana Islands, send your application to:

USCIS Lockbox Facility
USCIS
P.O. Box 21251
Phoenix, AZ 85036

Note: If you are overseas and filing an N-400, you should send your application to the Service Center that serves the USCIS office where you want to be interviewed. For example, if you want to be interviewed in the Honolulu office, you should send your application to the California Service Center.

Important! Look for your state. Where will you mail your N-400?

SOME QUESTIONS YOU MAY HAVE

What about my children?

Your natural or adopted children here with you may become citizens when you are naturalized, without filing any forms, if they are minors (under 18 years of age), unmarried, and legally admitted for permanent residence.

You may obtain a U.S. passport for your children as evidence of citizenship. If the children need further evidence of citizenship, you may submit an Application for Certificate of Citizenship (Form N-600).

I am not sure that I have *continuous* residence because I went back and forth to my native country during my mother's illness. Do I qualify?

If you have questions about your eligibility, you may want to seek advice from an immigration attorney or an immigrant assistance organization. Your local USCIS office can help you find one of these organizations.

Can I bring any of my family here?

As a permanent resident, you can petition for your spouse and unmarried children under age 21. When you become a citizen, you can do even more . . . much more.

What can I do if I lose any of my naturalization papers or change my name?

A person whose Certificate of Naturalization has been lost, mutilated, or destroyed or a naturalized person whose name has been changed by a court or by marriage *after* naturalization may apply for a new paper. The application form (N-565) is available from the USCIS Forms Line at 1-800-870-3676 or on the Internet at http://uscis.gov. It should be filled out, following the instructions on the form, and taken or mailed to the local USCIS office, along with the required photographs and a check or money order for $345 made out to the U.S. Department of Homeland Security. Any documents that show the reason for the change of status should be submitted.

NOTE: If a person changes his or her name or marital status, there is no legal requirement to apply for a new certificate. This is the person's option.

If a person loses a Permanent Resident Card (green card), he or she must file Form I-90. This form is also available from the USCIS Forms Line at 1-800-870-3676. Again it should be carefully filled out, following the instructions on the form, and submitted with a check or money order for $450 to that office.

What do I do if I move after I send in my N-400?
You must notify USCIS of your change of address within 10 days of your move.

- You can change your address online. Go to: *https://egov.uscis.gov/crisgwi/go?act.on-coa.Terms.*
- You can change your address on your pending N-400 by phone. You can call 1-800-375-5283 from 8 a.m. to 6 p.m., Monday to Friday.
- You must also change your address by mail. You can call 1-800-870-3676 or go online to http://uscis.gov to request Form AR-11 (Alien's Change of Address Card) and mail it to the office where you sent your Form N-400.

It is very important to notify USCIS of the new address. If you do not do so, USCIS will not send your notifications to the right place. For instance, you may not receive information on where and when to get fingerprinted and you may not be aware of the date and place of your interview.

Step 3—Getting Fingerprinted

After you file your application, the next step is to have your fingerprints taken. The USCIS will send you a letter that tells you where to go for fingerprinting. Usually, you will go to an Application Support Center.

When you go to the fingerprinting location, you must take with you your notice from the USCIS, your Permanent Resident Card, and another form of picture identification. The best form of identification is your passport.

The USCIS will send your fingerprints to the Federal Bureau of Investigation (FBI) for a criminal background check. While the FBI is doing the background check, the USCIS will be reviewing your N-400 file. The USCIS may find that it needs more documents from you before you can have your interview. If it needs more documents, the USCIS will send you a letter telling you what it needs and where you should send the information.

You can always check the status of your application online at *https://egov.uscis.gov/cris/Dashboard/CaseStatus.do*. You will need to have the number that came on the receipt that USCIS sent to you to let you know that they received your application.

After the background check is done and the USCIS has all the documents it needs, it will send you a notice that will tell you the date, time, and place of your interview.

Step 4—Going to Your Naturalization Interview

Some time after you file your N-400, you will be notified to go to be fingerprinted. Some time later, you will be called for the interview. It may take around five months to be scheduled for the naturalization interview. You will receive a notice in the mail telling you where and when to go for your interview. It is very important that you keep your appointment. If it is at a location that is unfamiliar to you, take a "practice" trip so that you will know how long it takes to get there. Do not try to change the date! But if you must do so, write a letter to the office where you are supposed to go, asking for a new date and giving the reason for your request. Then you will receive a new appointment. You do not need to bring anyone with you; witnesses are not required. You can bring your attorney or your legal service worker with you to the interview if you feel it is necessary. But you do need to bring whatever documents USCIS tells you to bring in the appointment notice. Be early! Allow extra time for security checks. If you do not show up on time, your case may be closed. Don't let that happen!

The office may be crowded and you may have to wait for your interview. Do not be impatient; keep calm! You have prepared for this test. You have nothing to worry about. Listen carefully to the examiner's questions. During the interview, your ability to understand and to speak English is also being tested. Answer all questions. Follow all instructions. Don't be nervous!

The examiner will have your file and may ask you questions about the N-400, possibly about your residence or your job experience, or why you want to become a citizen. You have reviewed such questions many times. Next will come the test of English and civics. You may be asked to read a passage like those in Reading Practice in this book. The examiner will also ask you about the government, history, and geography of the United States. If you do all the reading exercises in the book, you will know all that!

For the reading test, you will be asked to read a sentence out loud. You will have three opportunities to read a sentence out loud correctly. Each sentence has words from the list of reading vocabulary provided by USCIS. For example, you may be asked to read sentences such as:

1. The president lives in the White House.

2. George Washington was the father of our country.

3. Citizens have the right to vote.

4. How many states are in the United States?

5. Thanksgiving was our first holiday.

The reading vocabulary for the test is in the Appendix. Make sure you can pronounce all the words correctly.

For the writing test, you will be asked to write a sentence that the interviewer gives you. Again, you only need to do one correctly, and you will have three opportunities to complete the requirement. Each sentence has words from the list of writing vocabulary provided by USCIS. For example, you may be asked to write sentences such as:

1. The capital of the United States is Washington, D.C.

2. Independence Day is in July.

3. John Adams was our second president.

4. Canada is to the north of the United States.

5. There are 100 senators in Congress.

Get the idea? Write them now. Say the words as you write. The writing vocabulary for the test is in the Appendix.

For the American government, American history, and integrated civics items for the test, the examiner will ask you to answer (out loud) 10 of the 100 questions shown in the Appendix. You must answer 6 of the 10 questions correctly to pass the test.

By the way, if your English-speaking, -reading, and -writing abilities are already advanced, you may want to study only the reading vocabulary, writing vocabulary, and test questions in the Appendix, as well as the sections on what to expect from the application process.

Step 5—
Taking the Oath

After you pass the test and the USCIS approves your application, the last step is to attend a ceremony and take the Oath of Allegiance to the United States. The USCIS will send you a Notice of Naturalization Oath Ceremony (Form N-445), which will tell you the date and time of your ceremony.

If you can't attend the ceremony on that day, return the notice (Form N-445) to your local USCIS office. Include a letter that explains why you cannot be at the ceremony that day, and ask the USCIS to reschedule you.

Try to get to the ceremony early. There may be many other people being naturalized that day, and everyone has to check in before the ceremony begins. Remember: The naturalization ceremony is a meaningful event. The USCIS requests that you dress in proper attire (no jeans, shorts, or flip flops).

Bring your Permanent Resident Card (green card) with you. You will have to turn it in when you check in for the ceremony. You don't have to worry: You won't need the card anymore once you get your Certificate of Naturalization at the ceremony.

If more than a day has passed between your interview and the ceremony, you will need to answer several questions. The questions will be on the back of Form N-445 that the USCIS sent you. Read the questions and mark your answers before you get to the ceremony. *Answer the questions on the back of Form N-445 only for the time since your interview.*

At the ceremony, you will take the Oath of Allegiance to the United States. An official will read each part of the oath slowly and ask you to repeat the words.

The Oath of Allegiance

I hereby declare on oath,

that I absolutely and entirely renounce and abjure all allegiance and fidelity to any foreign prince, potentate, state, or sovereignty, of whom or which I have heretofore been a subject or citizen;

that I will support and defend the Constitution and laws of the United States of America against all enemies, foreign and domestic;

that I will bear true faith and allegiance to the same;

that I will bear arms on behalf of the United States when required by the law;

that I will perform noncombatant service in the Armed Forces of the United States when required by the law;

that I will perform work of national importance under civilian direction when required by the law; and that I take this obligation freely without any mental reservation or purpose of evasion; so help me God.

If you believe that you qualify for a modified oath because of your religious training and beliefs, you must send a letter to the USCIS along with your application for naturalization (Form N-400) explaining the situation.

Once you have taken the oath, you will receive your Certificate of Naturalization, proving that you are now a citizen of the United States.

Part
Three

PREPARING
FOR THE
TEST

Step 1—More Practice in Reading and Writing English

READING PRACTICE EXERCISE I

Practice your oral English by reading this passage aloud.

Good Moral Character

In general, good moral character means that you act in accordance with society's principles of right or good conduct and that you are honest and ethical. Good moral character means that you know the difference between right and wrong, that you choose to obey the laws of the United States and to observe the standards of your new country. The USCIS has given the following examples of things that might show a lack of good moral character:

- Illegal gambling
- Terrorist acts
- Drug or alcohol addiction
- Prostitution
- Criminal record during period of residence here or conviction for murder at any time
- Lying under oath in order to gain citizenship
- Polygamy (having more than one spouse at the same time)
- Failing to pay court-ordered child support or alimony payments
- Persecuting anyone because of race, religion, national origin, political opinion, or social group

It is important to answer all questions relating to this subject truthfully! If you do not tell the truth, the USCIS may deny your application.

It is important to note that if you have committed certain serious crimes, USCIS may decide to remove you from the United States. If you have questions, you may want to seek advice from an immigrant assistance organization or an immigration attorney before applying.

Except for the crimes of murder and aggravated felony, the requirement of good moral character refers to the immigrant's behavior during his or her period of residence here.

Read each question aloud. Answer by writing "yes" or "no" on the line next to the question.

1. Have you at any time, anywhere, ever ordered, incited, assisted, or otherwise participated in the persecution of any person because of race, religion, national origin, or political opinion? _____

    _____

2. Have you ever failed to comply with the Selective Service laws?_____

    _____

3. Since becoming a permanent resident, have you ever failed to file a federal income tax return? _____

    _____

4. Do you believe in the Constitution and form of government of the United States?_____

    _____

5. Have you ever given false testimony for the purpose of obtaining any immigration benefit? _____

    _____

Did you understand the questions?

Did you answer "no" to questions 1, 2, 3, and 5?

Did you answer "yes" to question 4?

You passed the test.

Practice saying these words:

assist   **service**   **participate**
persecute   **allegiance**

Look them up in the Word List in the Appendix.

READING PRACTICE EXERCISE II

Now test your progress in oral English by reading and answering the questions following the reading passages. Read aloud in front of a mirror or have someone listen to your pronunciation.

Who Can Be Naturalized?

Men and women who have entered the United States for permanent residence and who want to be citizens may apply for naturalization. Others have done it, and you can do it, too!

When we move from permanent resident to citizen, we become equal to people who were born here or who were naturalized before us. No one asks how or when! We can start the process if we are 18 years or older, were legally accepted for permanent residence, and have lived here for five or more years. There are some exceptions to the residence requirement; and I know they are based on the immigration laws.

The first step to naturalization is to obtain and fill out an Application for Naturalization (Form N-400) and then mail it with a check or money order for $680 (which includes the fingerprinting fee) to the appropriate regional office of the USCIS. And then wait!

1. What do the following words mean?

application	**exception**	**newcomer**
apply	**ineligible**	**requirement**
basis	**lawfully**	**residence**
eligibility	**legally**	**resident**
eligible	**naturalization**	

    How did you do?
    Check your answers with the Word List in the Appendix.

2. Use each of the above words in a sentence.

    For example: The *basis* for my *eligibility* is five years as a permanent *resident* of the United States.

    Here, three words were used in the same sentence. Can you do the same? If you have difficulty, go back to Part One to find how the words were used there.

    _____

    _____

    _____

_____

_____

_____

_____

_____

_____

_____

_____

_____

_____

WRITING PRACTICE

Write the following sentences, completing those that have blanks for answer choices.

1. I want to be an American citizen. _____

_____

2. George Washington is called "the father of our country." _____

_____

3. Lincoln was our president during the Civil War. _____

_____

4. American Indians lived here before the Europeans came._____

_____

5. _____ is the capital of the United States.

6. There are 13 stripes and 50 stars on our flag. _____

_____

7. There are three colors in our flag: red, white, and blue. _____

_____

8. There are fifty (50) states in the United States. _____

_____

9. Citizens have the right to vote. _____

_____

10. Canada is to the north of the United States. _____

_____

11. Mexico is south of the United States. _____

_____

12. Congress makes our laws. _____

_____

13. I can read, write, and speak simple English. _____

_____

14. Thanksgiving is in November. _____

_____

15. John Adams was our second president. _____

_____

16. Columbus Day is in the month of October. _____

_____

17. Labor Day is in September. _____

_____

18. Independence Day is in the month of _____.

_____

19. Presidents' Day is in February. _____

_____

20. Memorial Day is in the month of May. _____

_____

REVIEW: MORE WRITING PRACTICE

Read each question carefully. Then write your answers in the spaces provided. Read your answer out loud to see if it makes sense. You can check what you wrote with the answers at the bottom of this page.

1. In your own words, write the answer to the question "What is

naturalization?" _____

_____

_____

_____

2. In your own words, write the answer to the question "Why is it important for

me to go through the naturalization process?" _____

_____

_____

_____

_____

_____

_____

_____

Now turn the book upside down and compare your answers with the answers given below. If you left something out, write the answer again, either below this sentence, or on another sheet of paper. If you wrote the answer using different words, you may still be correct. However, the main meaning of these answers must be the same. If not, write both question and correct answer on a separate sheet of paper.

ACCEPTABLE ANSWERS

1. Naturalization is the process of becoming a citizen, or the act of going from *alien to citizen.*

2. I want to be able to *vote.* I also think it is important to get an American *passport,* and to help some of my relatives come into the United States of America so our family is not separated. It may also enable me to apply for a government job or to *be elected* to public office. And it will not be necessary for me to show a *card* to prove that I belong here!

Step 2—Civics, History, and Geography

Part One included the *main requirements* for naturalization. There are also two *educational requirements* for naturalization.

The *first educational requirement* is that you understand English and be able to read, write, and speak words in ordinary use. Remember: Only those persons who are physically unable to do this, or persons older than 50 years old who have lived in the United States as permanent residents for more than 20 years, or who are older than 55 with more than 15 years of residence, are excused from this requirement. You have already had practice in reading and writing words needed to meet this educational requirement.

Now, you will also learn the facts that you need in order to meet the *second educational requirement* for naturalization: to demonstrate a knowledge and understanding of the history, geography, and principles and form of government of the United States (civics). An applicant who has a physical or developmental disability or a mental impairment may be exempt from this requirement.

Note: This is a self-help book. While you are learning important facts, each unit aims to help you improve your English. Pay attention to words and their meaning while you read and learn the content in this section. You will learn all you need to know—and much more!

OUR GOVERNMENT

Our government is a **democracy.** That means it is a government of the people, by the people, and for the people. It is a government by the elected representatives of all the voters. It is a *tripartite* government, which means it has three parts, or branches—the legislative, the executive, and the judicial.

Our government is also a **republic.** This means that the supreme power is given to representatives elected by popular vote of all citizens.

You see that democracy and republic mean almost the same thing. Long ago, in small units of government, citizens got together and made the laws for their communities. That is the real meaning of democracy. Today that kind of democracy exists only in a few small towns in the northeastern part of our country. Through town meetings, all of the voters decide on what is to be done in their town.

Of course, this is not possible where a great many people live. Today, we make our voices heard by voting for people to represent us. The two largest political parties in the United States, the Democratic and the Republican parties, derive their names from *democracy* and *republic;* so it should not be difficult to remember these words.

Our country is a **federation,** or association, of states. The government for the whole country is, therefore, called the *federal government*. The plan for this government is set by the Constitution, the supreme law of our land.

The above paragraphs describe the *form* of government. Other characteristics describe our country as well. One of these is our *economic system*. We have a capitalist or market economy, which means that ownership and investments are mainly by individuals and corporations, not by the government.

THE CONSTITUTION: A LAW FOR ALL SEASONS

The **Constitution** is the highest law of the United States. It has an opening statement, or Preamble, that says, "WE THE PEOPLE of the United States, in order to form a more perfect Union, establish justice, insure domestic tranquility, provide for the common defense, promote the general welfare, and secure the blessings of liberty to ourselves and our posterity, do ordain and establish this Constitution for the United States of America." The Preamble is followed by seven Articles that describe how the government works. The Constitution was adopted in 1789 as the supreme law of the land. At that time, there were only 13 states (the 13 original colonies).

The leaders of the country changed it by adding 10 amendments known as the Bill of Rights in 1791. The Bill of Rights is very important because it protects the rights of all Americans, rights that cannot be taken away from us. Since that time other amendments, or changes, have been made as needs arise. The Fifth Article of the Constitution tells how this can be done:

> **The Congress, whenever two-thirds of both Houses shall deem it necessary, shall propose amendments to this Constitution, or, on the application of the legislatures of two-thirds of the several States, shall call a convention for proposing amendments, which in either case shall be valid to all intents and purposes, as part of this Constitution, when ratified by the legislatures of three-fourths of the several States, or by conventions in three-fourths thereof, as the one or the other mode of ratification may be proposed by the Congress; provided that no amendment which may be made prior to the year one thousand eight hundred and eight shall in any manner affect the first and fourth clauses in the ninth section of the first article; and that no State, without its consent, shall be deprived of its equal suffrage in the Senate.**

It is not easy, but this procedure has been followed 27 times. The result is that the Constitution is kept up to date.

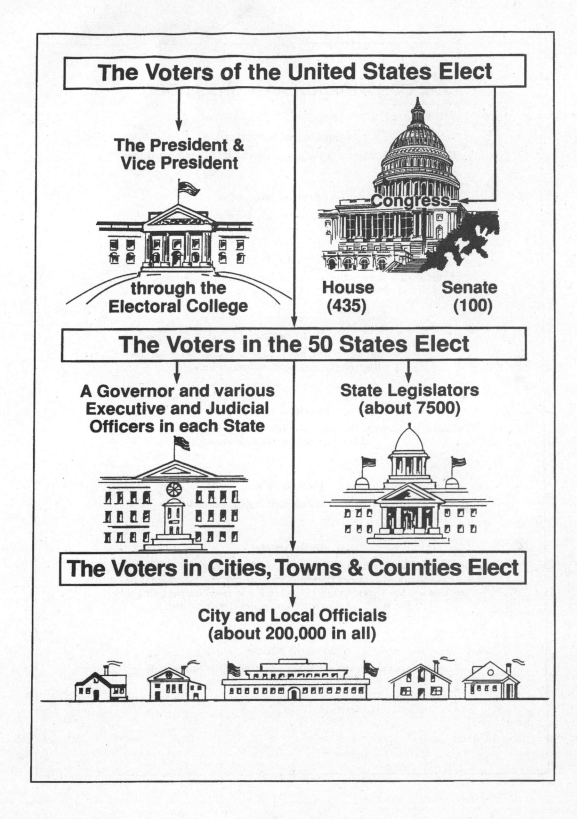

Figure 5

Source: U.S. Department of Justice, Immigration and Naturalization Service

THE CONSTITUTION AS IT WAS ADOPTED

Preamble (Introduction)

Explains the purposes of the people in adopting the Constitution.

First Article

Provides for a Congress and defines its power to make laws.

Second Article

Provides for the election of a president and vice president, with
defined powers, and for the *appointment* of other officials.

Third Article

Sets up a Supreme Court, authorizes the Congress to set up
other courts, and defines their powers.

Fourth Article

Defines relationships between the federal government and the States,
and between the States themselves.

Fifth Article

Tells how the Constitution may be amended.

Sixth Article

Accepts responsibility for all debts that the Nation owed before the adoption
of the Constitution; declares that the Constitution, constitutional laws, and
treaties are the supreme law of the land; and provides that all public
officers must take an oath to support the Constitution.

Seventh Article

Declares that ratification (approval) by nine States will
put the Constitution into effect.

Figure 6

Source: U.S. Department of Justice, Immigration and Naturalization Service

THE BILL OF RIGHTS—1791

First Amendment

Forbids the Congress to interfere with religion, free speech, a free press, or with the right to *assemble* peaceably, or to petition the government.

Second Amendment

Guarantees to the people the right to have weapons.

Third Amendment

Guarantees against lodging soldiers in private houses without the *consent* of the owners.

Fourth Amendment

Provides that there shall be no search or *seizure* of persons, houses, goods, or papers, without a *warrant.*

Fifth Amendment

Declares that there shall be no *trial* for serious offenses without a *grand jury indictment,* no repeated trials for the same offense, no *condemnation* without trial, no compulsion to be a *witness* against oneself, and no property taken for public use except at a fair price.

Sixth Amendment

Requires a speedy and public trial for criminal offenses in the district where the crime was committed, a fair jury, a plain statement of the *accusation,* gives the *accused* the right to be represented by a lawyer and to *compel* the attendance of his witnesses, and requires all witnesses to *testify* in the presence of the accused.

Seventh Amendment

Provides that in *lawsuits* about anything valued at more than $20, a trial by jury shall be allowed.

Eighth Amendment

Prohibits too large *bail* or *fines,* and cruel or unusual *punishments.*

Ninth Amendment

Declares that rights not stated in the Constitution are not therefore taken away from the people.

Tenth Amendment

States that powers not delegated to the United States nor prohibited by the Constitution to the States are reserved to the States or to the people.

Figure 7

Source: U.S. Department of Justice, Immigration and Naturalization Service

AMENDMENTS PASSED AFTER THE BILL OF RIGHTS

Eleventh Amendment (1795)
A citizen of one state, or an alien, cannot sue another state in a federal court.

Twelfth Amendment (1804)
Electors must vote for president and vice president separately.

Thirteenth Amendment (1865)
Ended slavery.

Fourteenth Amendment (1868)
All persons born or naturalized in the United States are citizens.

Fifteenth Amendment (1870)
No person can be kept from voting because of race or color.

Sixteenth Amendment (1913)
Congress has the power to put a tax on money earned by the people.

Seventeenth Amendment (1913)
Senators are to be elected by the people.

Eighteenth Amendment (1919)
Prohibited the making, selling, or transportation of intoxicating liquor.

Nineteenth Amendment (1920)
No person can be kept from voting because of being a woman.

Twentieth Amendment (1933)
The president, the vice president, and the Congress shall take office in January.

Twenty-first Amendment (1933)
Did away with the Eighteenth Amendment.

Twenty-second Amendment (1951)
The same person cannot be elected president more than twice.

Twenty-third Amendment (1961)
Citizens living in the District of Columbia can vote for
president and vice president.

Twenty-fourth Amendment (1964)
Citizens cannot be made to pay a tax to vote for the president,
the vice president, or members of the Congress.

Twenty-fifth Amendment (1967)
The vice president becomes acting president when the president is disabled.

Twenty-sixth Amendment (1971)
A citizen shall not be denied the right to vote because of age
if he is 18 years of age or older.

Twenty-seventh Amendment (1992)
Compensation for the services of Senators and Representatives
shall not be changed until an election is held.

Figure 8

Source: U.S. Department of Justice, Immigration and Naturalization Service

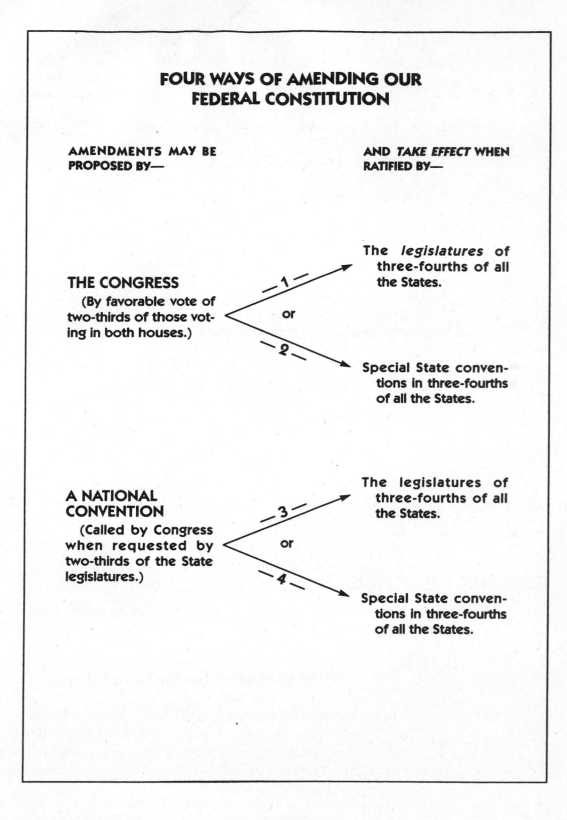

Figure 9

Source: U.S. Department of Justice, Immigration and Naturalization Service

REVIEW

Supply the missing words in the following blanks.

1. The_____describes the plan of our government.

2. The first three words of the Constitution establish the idea of self-government. These words are _____.

3. The Constitution was_____in 1789.

4. At that time there were_____states in the United States.

5. These states are sometimes called the original _____.

6. The Constitution protects the rights of all _____today.

Answer this question in the space provided.

7. If a group of people wanted to introduce an amendment to the Constitution making it illegal to carry guns, what would they have to do?

_____

_____

_____

See the answer key on page 182.

READING PRACTICE

Practice your oral English by reading the passage below. Then check your understanding by writing about what you have read in the spaces provided.

The Government of the United States

The government of the United States of America is a democracy, a government of the people, by the people, and for the people. It is a tripartite government because it has three parts, or branches. (*Tri* means "three.") You know that a triangle has three sides. In the same way, our government has three branches.

These branches are the legislative, or law-making; the executive; and the judicial. The executive branch carries out the laws. The judicial branch judges laws.

The plan of our government is in the Constitution, the highest law of the land. When the Constitution was first written, the leaders of the new country left out the rights of the people. This was an oversight for the citizens wanting a guarantee that their rights would be protected. And so, the first 10 amendments to the Constitution were adopted to do just that. They are called the Bill of Rights.

These rights are listed on page 65. Read them again! Then write a summary of them in your own words on the lines below. Check to see how your summary agrees with paragraph numbers three and four on pages 69 and 70.

_____

_____

_____

_____

_____

_____

_____

_____

_____

SUMMARY: HOW THE BILL OF RIGHTS PROTECTS AMERICANS

1. The first 10 amendments to the Constitution are called the Bill of Rights.

2. These rights are guaranteed by the Constitution, the Supreme (highest) law of our land, and are protected by the Supreme Court, the highest court of our land. The amendments were adopted in 1791 and now are older than 200 years old. They are still used to protect us.

3. The First Amendment protects freedom of religion, of speech, and of the press; the right to assemble peacefully and to petition (ask) the government to set right or cancel a law that denies them their rights. The Fourth Amendment guarantees that no one will come into your house to search it without a warrant. And we have the right to bear arms (carry guns) to protect ourselves (Second Amendment) as well as the right to a fair trial if we are accused of a crime (Sixth Amendment). The last amendment, the 10th, states that any power not given to the federal government is a power of the state or the people. (We will read more about this in the section on state and local governments.)

4. Sometimes, we hear of a witness in a court trial, "taking the Fifth." This refers to the Fifth Amendment, "no person shall be compelled to be a witness against himself, nor be deprived of life, liberty or property without due process of law."

5. Another important guarantee of "due process" is in the Fourteenth Amendment, which was adopted in 1868 after the Civil War. The Fourteenth Amendment also tells us the meaning of the word citizen:

> All persons born or naturalized in the United States, and subject to its jurisdiction [authority] are citizens of the United States, and of the state where they reside. . .

REVIEW

Write your answers to these two questions in the blank spaces.

1. The first 10 amendments to the Constitution are called _____.

2. The First Amendment guarantees freedom of _____, _____, and _____. It protects the rights _____

   and _____.

See the answer key on page 182.

THE FEDERAL GOVERNMENT: FORM AND STRUCTURE

The Constitution broadly outlines the form and structure of the federal government. Details of operation and management have been worked out over the years since 1789, so that what we have today is a workable system of government for 50 states.

The writers of the Constitution set up the government in such a way that no person, or group of persons, would have too much power. Our system of government is based on two principles: the *separation of powers* and a system of *checks and balances*. Let us see what these principles mean.

The government is divided into three branches—the legislative, the executive, and the judicial—each with separate functions.

The **legislative branch,** or **Congress,** makes the laws. It is composed of a Senate and a House of Representatives. Two senators are elected from each state, each for a six-year term; representatives are elected for terms of two years. The number of representatives each state has is determined by the size of its population.

The **executive branch** is headed by the president, who is elected for a term of four years. A vice president is elected at the same time and from the same political party. The Constitution tells how a president may be removed from office. It provides that upon such removal or upon the death of the president, the vice president takes office. If the vice president is also removed from office, or dies, the speaker of the House of Representatives would take office as president of the United States.

The third branch of the federal government is the judicial branch. Its function is to interpret the laws. To do this, there is a network of federal courts, the highest of which is the Supreme Court.

Briefly, this explains the **separation of powers.** Now let us see how the **system of checks and balances** works.

Each of the three branches of government has been set up to check the other branches. For example, the president must sign into law all bills passed by Congress; if he thinks that a bill is not good, he can veto or say no to that bill. Then the bill must go back to Congress. It can only be passed by a two-thirds vote of both houses of Congress after the president's veto.

The president appoints many high government officials, his cabinet, head of agencies, and federal judges (even those of the Supreme Court). But all of these appointments must be approved by the Senate. This is one way the legislative branch checks the executive branch.

In this process, the judicial branch has the "last word" over the other two branches. The Supreme Court may decide that a law made by Congress and signed by the president is unconstitutional; that is, it is not in accordance with the Constitution. There is no appeal from a decision of the Supreme Court!

REVIEW

Do you know what these words mean? Write the meaning next to the word. If you are not sure, look up the meaning in the Word List in the Appendix.

1. judicial _____

2. interpret_____

3. Senate _____

4. House of Representatives _____

5. separation of powers_____

6. system of checks and balances_____

7. legislative_____

8. executive_____

From the list of new words in items 1–8, choose the words that fit in the blanks in sentences 9–13.

9. Two principles on which our government is based are_____ and

_____.

10. The _____ branch is made up of two houses, the

_____ and the _____.

11. The _____ branch carries out the laws.

12. If the president dies or is unable to perform his duties, the _____

_____ becomes president.

13. The _____ branch, made up of a series of courts,

_____ the law.

See the answer key on page 182.

Congress: Your Representatives

The legislative branch of the federal government is called the **Congress,** which, according to the Constitution, has power to make laws for the nation. The Constitution also sets the qualifications for senators and representatives and tells how they are to be elected.

At the present time, there are **100 senators (two from each of the 50 states) and 435 representatives apportioned according to population.** In the Senate both of the senators from your state represent you, but in the House of Representatives only the representative from the district where you live represents you.

The function of Congress is to make laws, but nowhere in the Constitution is there a statement of the exact steps that must be taken in the law-making process. The steps by which a bill introduced by a senator or a representative becomes a law have developed over the years. In fact, the whole committee system, so important in the law-making process, was set up by Congress in order to handle its business more efficiently.

Congress begins its sessions on January 3 of each year and is in session until the members of both Houses vote to **adjourn,** or close, the meeting. Each of the houses has its own chairperson: The vice president presides over the Senate; the speaker of the House of Representatives is chosen by the members of that body and presides over all of its sessions.

Congress has many important powers: to coin money, to set taxes and collect them, to declare war, and (a very important power to you) to establish the requirements for naturalization. It has many other powers, and each of the houses has some special powers: for example, all bills relating to money must be proposed in the House of Representatives and passed there before going to the Senate. The Senate alone has the power to **ratify,** or approve, a treaty made with a foreign country.

Sometimes you hear the word *bill* used to describe an act being considered by Congress. Do you know the difference between a bill and a law? A **bill** is a formal proposal recommended by a member of Congress. Thousands of bills are introduced in Congress each year, but many do not become laws because, after consideration by committees or by the full House, they are not approved. Even after a bill is approved by a majority vote in both houses, it must be signed by the president. If the president vetoes the bill, it returns to Congress where it must be passed by a two-thirds vote. Only then does it become a **law!**

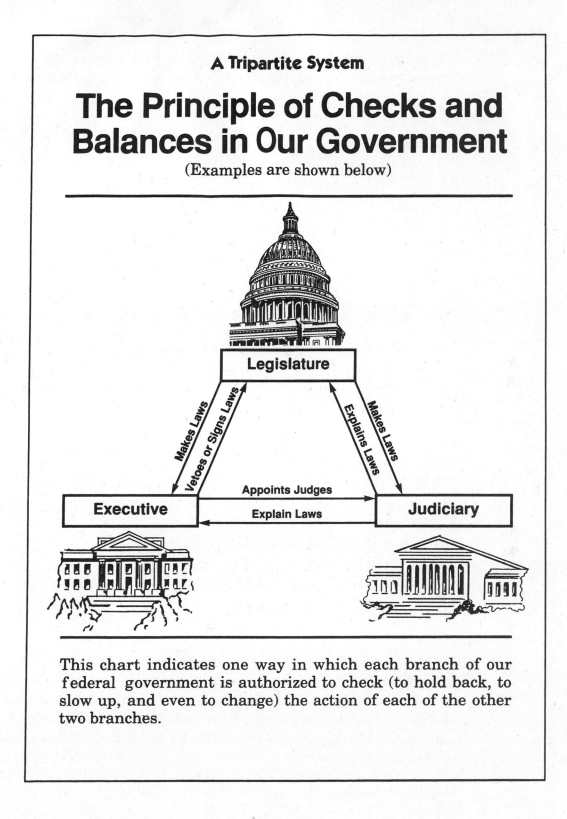

A Tripartite System

The Principle of Checks and Balances in Our Government

(Examples are shown below)

This chart indicates one way in which each branch of our federal government is authorized to check (to hold back, to slow up, and even to change) the action of each of the other two branches.

Figure 10

Source: U.S. Department of Justice, Immigration and Naturalization Service

REVIEW

Do you know what these words mean? Write the meanings next to the words. If you are not sure, look up the meaning in the Word List in the Appendix.

1. qualification _____

2. apportion _____

3. adjourn _____

4. ratify _____

5. treaty _____

6. majority _____

Now, write the answers to the following questions in the space provided.

7. Why does the Congress have two houses? _____

_____

8. Can you introduce a bill in Congress? _____

_____

9. When does Congress begin each session? _____

_____

10. When does Congress adjourn? _____

_____

11. How does a bill become a law? _____

_____

Note the following paragraph.

    An English writer once said that the men who founded the United States had a clear idea of what they wanted to put into the Constitution and then left it to later generations to work out the details. He added that this plan has been remarkably successful.

12. In your own words, write one example of this.

_____

_____

_____

See the answer key on page 183.

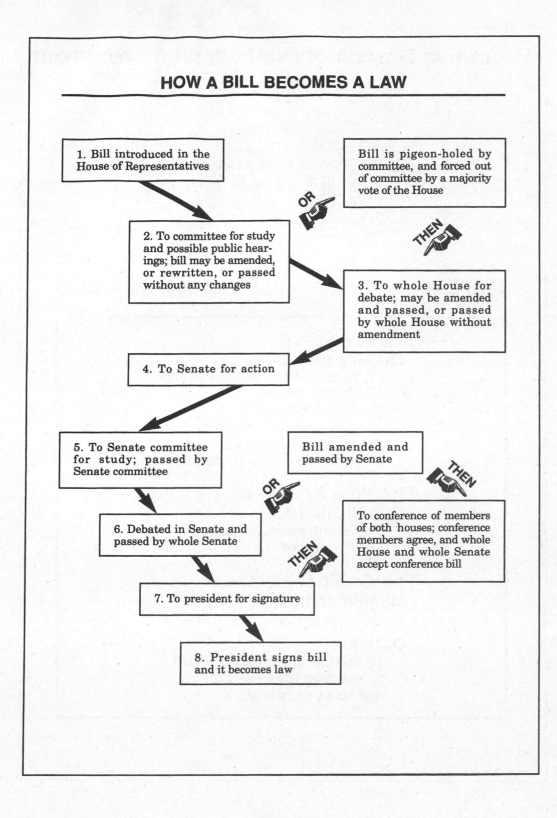

Figure 11

Source: U.S. Department of Justice, Immigration and Naturalization Service

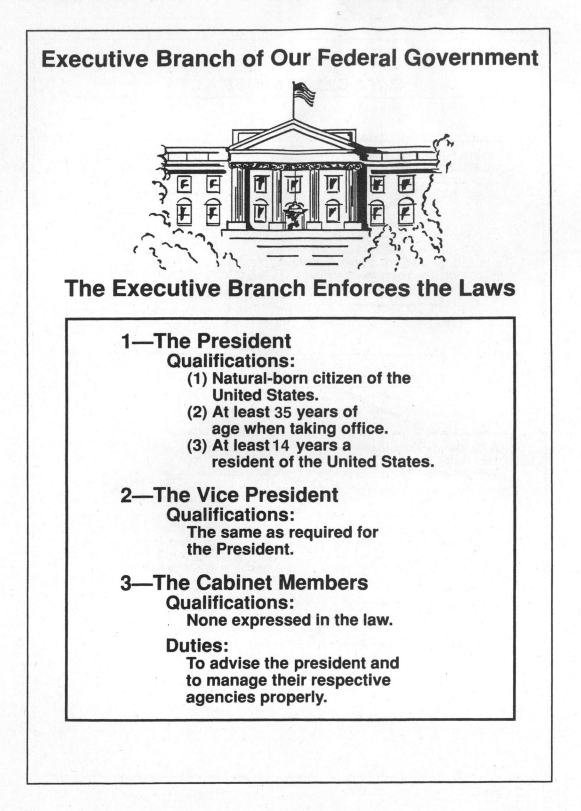

Executive Branch of Our Federal Government

The Executive Branch Enforces the Laws

1—The President
Qualifications:
(1) Natural-born citizen of the United States.
(2) At least 35 years of age when taking office.
(3) At least 14 years a resident of the United States.

2—The Vice President
Qualifications:
The same as required for the President.

3—The Cabinet Members
Qualifications:
None expressed in the law.

Duties:
To advise the president and to manage their respective agencies properly.

Figure 12

Source: U.S. Department of Justice, Immigration and Naturalization Service

The President

Term of office—4 years.
Salary—$400,000 a year.
Election—November of every fourth year.
Inauguration—January 20 following election.
Elected—By the people through the Electoral College.
Qualifications—Natural-born citizen at least 35 years old and at least 14 years a resident of the United States.

Succession to the office—(People next in line to be president if the president cannot carry out his or her duties.)
1. Vice President.
2. Speaker of the House of Representatives.
3. President <u>pro tempore</u> of the Senate.
4. Secretary of State.
5. Secretary of the Treasury.
6. Secretary of Defense.
7. Attorney General.
8. Secretary of the Interior.
9. Secretary of Agriculture.
10. Secretary of Commerce.
11. Secretary of Labor.
12. Secretary of Health and Human Services.
13. Secretary of Homeland Security.
14. Secretary of Housing and Urban Development.
15. Secretary of Transportation.
16. Secretary of Energy.
17. Secretary of Education.
18. Secretary of Veterans' Affairs.

Chief power and duty—To enforce the Constitution, the laws made by the Congress, and treaties.

Other powers—
1. To veto bills.
2. To recommend bills to the Congress.
3. To call special sessions of the Congress.
4. To deliver messages to the Congress.
5. To appoint federal judges.
6. To appoint representatives to foreign countries.
7. To appoint department heads and other important officials.
8. To pardon.
9. To carry on official business with foreign nations.
10. To be commander-in-chief of the armed forces.

Figure 13

Source: U.S. Department of Justice, Immigration and Naturalization Service

The Presidency

The president is the **chief executive,** or head, of the federal government. His or her job is to carry out the laws and to manage the affairs of the country. Only the president and the vice president can be voted for by all the citizens of the United States. Our president through 2016 is Barack Obama. Joe Biden is our vice president. In January 2017 there will be a new president and vice president. Be sure to learn their names. Both are elected for terms of four years and cannot serve for more than two terms, as provided in Amendment 22 of the Constitution.

The president and his family live in the White House, at 1600 Pennsylvania Avenue, Washington, D.C., a building that symbolizes the dignity of the office. The president also has his office here. If you write a letter to the president, you should address him as Mr. President.

The president takes the oath of office on January 20 following his or her election. Just as your Oath of Allegiance will be administered by a judge when you become a citizen, the president's oath is administered by a judge—the highest ranking judge in the country, the **chief justice of the Supreme Court.** John Roberts is the present chief justice.

Here is the oath that the president takes.

PRESIDENTIAL OATH OF OFFICE

I do solemnly swear that I will faithfully execute the office of President of the United States, and will to the best of my ability, preserve, protect and defend the Constitution of the United States.

Because the president has many important responsibilities, he or she appoints people to help him or her. These people, each heading an executive department, make up the Cabinet. All Cabinet members must be approved by the Senate before they can serve. Remember, this is part of our system of checks and balances! Following are the Cabinet members and their duties:

Cabinet Members

POSITION	DUTIES
Attorney General	heads the Department of Justice and represents the government in all legal matters.
Secretary of Agriculture	manages farming and the improvement of conditions among farmers.
Secretary of Commerce	manages trade relations between the United States and other countries and helps business people.
Secretary of Defense	manages the armed services (Army, Navy, Air Force, and Marines).
Secretary of Education	supervises special programs of education authorized by the Congress.
Secretary of Energy	coordinates the work of agencies relating to the development of power.
Secretary of Health and Human Services	is in charge of the common needs of the people, including Social Security, child labor, and public health and assistance.
Secretary of Homeland Security	coordinates border and transportation security, protects critical infrastructure, and provides protection from chemical and biological threats. Heads U.S. Citizenship and Immigration Services.
Secretary of Housing and Urban Development	handles the financing and construction of public housing.
Secretary of the Interior	takes care of all public lands.
Secretary of Labor	manages the conditions of working people.
Secretary of State	has charge of all foreign affairs.
Secretary of Transportation	coordinates different kinds of transportation: aviation, highways, railroads, and so on.
Secretary of the Treasury	has charge of federal funds and taxes.
Secretary of Veterans' Affairs	oversees programs and advises president.

Now you know what heavy responsibilities may rest with the president and his advisers (the Cabinet).

What about the vice president? As you may remember, he or she presides over the Senate at all of its sessions. That is an important responsibility. But probably the vice president's most important duty is to become president if the president dies, resigns, or is removed from office.

The first president of the United States was George Washington. His birthday, in February, is a national holiday. George Washington commanded the army during the American Revolution and brought a group of inexperienced, poorly equipped soldiers to victory. When the Constitution was written, it provided that one of the duties of the president was to be commander-in-chief of the armed forces.

Another president whose birthday is a holiday, at least in some parts of the country, is Abraham Lincoln, who served during the Civil War and who is credited with saving the Union and freeing the slaves with the Emancipation Proclamation.

REVIEW

Do you know what these words mean? Write the meanings next to the words. If you are not sure, look up the meaning in the Word List in the Appendix.

1. chief executive _____

2. oath _____

3. commerce _____

4. energy _____

5. treasury _____

6. Cabinet _____

7. agriculture _____

8. urban _____

9. attorney _____

Now write the answers to the following questions in the space provided.

10. Is the president's most important duty to make the laws or to

carry them out?_____

_____

11. Does the president have many responsibilities or a few responsibilities?____

_____

12. Who helps the president? _____

_____

13. Can a naturalized citizen become president of the United States?

_____

14. What oath does the president take? When does he take it?_____

_____

See the answer key on page 183.

Meet the Presidents

From the time the first president, often called "the father of our country," took office in 1789, to the present time, there have been 44 presidents of the United States. The term of office of a president is four years, but some presidents have served more than one term. The longest was FDR, or Franklin D. Roosevelt, who was elected for four terms but served only three. At Franklin Roosevelt's death in 1945, Vice President Truman took his place, and then was elected president in his own right.

Here are our presidents. Brief summaries of the events of their administrations follow.

1789–1797 GEORGE WASHINGTON

Offices of Secretary of State, Secretary of Treasury, Postmaster General, and Attorney General set up; Thomas Jefferson as Secretary of State, Alexander Hamilton as Secretary of Treasury, John Jay and James Monroe appointed ambassadors to London and Paris respectively. Congress votes a tariff and excise taxes to pay off federal debt. The Bill of Rights is ratified, the Bank of the United States is set up, public lands are sold to raise funds, a law mandates that the capital would be no further north than the Potomac River. Treaties are signed with England and Spain. In his farewell address, in 1796, President Washington warns against entangling foreign alliances and political party strife.

1798–1801 JOHN ADAMS (Federalist)

Department of Navy set up. Naturalization Act, Alien Act passed by Congress.

1801–1809 THOMAS JEFFERSON (Democratic-Republican)

Supreme Court landmark decision in case of *Marbury v. Madison*, Louisiana Purchase, expansion westward, Lewis and Clark expedition explores Northwest Territory.

1809–1817 JAMES MADISON (Democratic-Republican)

War of 1812 against England, Treaty of Ghent (1815). End of Federalist Party, which had opposed the War of 1812.

1817–1825 JAMES MONROE (Democratic-Republican)

Era of Good Feeling, Monroe Doctrine.

1825–1829 JOHN QUINCY ADAMS (National Republican)

The son of the second president. The Erie Canal; New York City becomes important seaport, Noah Webster publishes his *Dictionary*, which became the authority on language, thus helping national unity.

1829–1837 ANDREW JACKSON (Democrat)

Builds the Democratic Party. War with American Indians.

1837–1841 MARTIN VAN BUREN (Democrat)

Depression and financial panic. The Panic of 1837, supposedly caused by land speculation and overextension, results in high unemployment and poverty.

1841 WILLIAM HENRY HARRISON
Dies one month after being inaugurated; replaced by the vice president, John Tyler.

1841–1845 JOHN TYLER (Democrat)
First vice president to succeed to the presidency. First telegraph message sent from Baltimore to Washington. Borders of the country on the North (Canada) and South (Mexico) being discussed.

1845–1849 JAMES K. POLK (Democrat)
Annexation of Texas; Texas enters the Union as a slave state. War breaks out. The Mexican War is a victory for the United States. That, plus the purchase of vast lands in the Southwest from Mexico, makes this a very large country.

1849–1850 ZACHARY TAYLOR (Whig)
Beginning of the Whig Party, which later became the Republican Party. California Gold Rush, Forty-niners stampede westward. President dies, to be succeeded by vice president, Millard Fillmore.

1850–1853 MILLARD FILLMORE (Whig)
Compromise of 1850 (admission of free and slave states) prevents the breakup of the Union, *Uncle Tom's Cabin* published.

1853–1857 FRANKLIN PIERCE (Democrat)
Prosperity and peace, but slavery still an important factor in the division of the North and South. Kansas-Nebraska Bill realigns states on issue of slavery; this helps. Japan open to world trade.

1857–1861 JAMES BUCHANAN (Democrat)
Supreme Court landmark decision—*Dred Scott,* Lincoln-Douglas debates, Lincoln wins by a very small margin, and is elected.

1861–1865 ABRAHAM LINCOLN (Republican)
Civil War, Emancipation Proclamation effective January 1, 1863, surrender of Lee in 1865 ends war, Homestead Act, sale of Western land, establishment of land-grant colleges. President assassinated by John Wilkes Booth, April 14, 1865.

1865–1869 ANDREW JOHNSON (Republican)
Reconstruction period; Federal Army sent to the South to keep order; Thirteenth Amendment to the Constitution abolishes slavery forever, Purchase of Alaska, Fourteenth Amendment to the Constitution, equal rights for former slaves, institutes due process of law; civil rights. President impeached by the House of Representatives, tried by the Senate, found not guilty.

1869–1877 ULYSSES S. GRANT (Republican)
Railways extended cross-country, Depression, and Panic, Electoral Commission established. Corruption rampant. Fifteenth Amendment, giving freed men the right to vote, ratified.

1877–1881 RUTHERFORD B. HAYES (Republican)

Elected by Congress despite the fact that a Democrat won the popular vote. Prosperity followed by Depression. Indian rebellion put down; Indians forced to live on reservations. Federal army withdrawn from Southern states. Political corruption—the Tweed Ring in New York City (Tammany Hall). Railroad workers strike.

1881 JAMES GARFIELD (Republican)

Assassinated after six months in office, Replaced by vice president, Chester Arthur.

1881–1885 CHESTER ARTHUR (Republican)

Chinese Exclusion Act passed, first Civil Service Reform Bill enacted, rise of Big Business, disputes between labor and management grows.

1885–1889 GROVER CLEVELAND (Democrat)

Civil Service reform extended—pensions. Reduction in tariffs. Union workers riot in Chicago. AFL (American Federation of Labor) formed.

1889–1893 BENJAMIN HARRISON (Republican)

Grandson of William Henry Harrison. Idaho, Montana, North and South Dakota, Washington (state), and Wyoming admitted to the Union. Sherman Anti-Trust Act passed to control monopolies. Sherman Silver Act passed to permit free coinage of silver with its value fixed at a high level in relation to gold.

1893–1897 GROVER CLEVELAND (Democrat) Second Term

Depression and Panic of 1893 followed by good times and recognition of the United States as a world power. The gold standard and tariff become issues. Hard times for farmers.

1897–1901 WILLIAM McKINLEY (Republican)

Spanish-American War brought on by native rebellion against Spanish rule in Cuba. Treaty of Paris, 1898—Puerto Rico, the Philippines, and Guam become American possessions. Hawaiian Islands annexed. America seen as great naval power. Formation of Pan-American Union. President McKinley reelected for a second term, but six months later, he is assassinated, replaced by the vice president, Theodore Roosevelt.

1901–1909 THEODORE ROOSEVELT (Republican)

Acquisition of the Panama Canal Zone, the result of a revolt by Panama from Colombia. Settlement of Russo-Japanese War. America seen as a great world power. On the domestic scene, a coal miners' strike is settled, Departments of Labor and Commerce established. The "Rough Rider" president, as he was called, is reelected.

1909–1913 WILLIAM HOWARD TAFT (Republican)

Tariff Reform policy defeated. Sixteenth Amendment to the Constitution ratified, establishing an income tax. Antitrust suits against Standard Oil Company and American Tobacco Company instituted.

1913–1921 WOODROW WILSON (Democrat)

Seventeenth Amendment to the Constitution ratified, providing for the direct election of senators. Federal Trade Commission created to prevent unfair competition. Federal Reserve Act regulating banks passed. When war breaks out in Europe, the president declares America to be neutral, but in 1917 diplomatic relations with Germany are broken off over threats of submarine warfare. Congress declares war on April 6, 1917; Amercan troops and supplies are mobilized. Germany signs an armistice on November 11, 1918, ending the war. The Treaty of Versailles signals the League of Nations, the 14 Points for Peace, not adopted. 1919 sees the adoption of the Eighteenth Amendment, women's suffrage, and the Nineteenth Amendment, Prohibition.

1921–1923 WARREN HARDING (Republican)

Period of prosperity and corruption. The president dies in 1923 to be succeeded by the vice president, Calvin Coolidge.

1923–1929 CALVIN COOLIDGE (Republican)

Teapot Dome Scandal. Industrial prosperity, gambling on the stock market rises. The president chooses to not run again.

1929–1933 HERBERT HOOVER (Republican)

Stock market crash, leading to terrible Depression; factories close, banks fail, millions lose jobs, no relief for the needy.

1933–1945 FRANKLIN DELANO ROOSEVELT (Democrat)

The New Deal. Establishment of CCC (Civilian Conservation Corps) and WPA (Works Progress Administration) puts jobless to work. The Social Security Act passed. FDR reelected by large margin. World War II declared, resulting in Selective Service Act, the first peacetime draft in United States. Pearl Harbor, December 7, 1941—The United States declares war on Japan on December 8, and on December 11, Germany and Italy declare war on the United States. Dwight Eisenhower made Supreme Commander of AEF forces. 1944—D-Day, June 6. President, reelected for fourth time, dies April 12, 1945, to be succeeded by vice president, Harry Truman.

1945–1953 HARRY S. TRUMAN (Democrat)

V-E Day, May 6, 1945, victory in Europe. Atomic bombs dropped on Hiroshima and Nagasaki, resulting in end of war. V-J Day, August 15, 1945, victory over Japan. Formation of United Nations at conference in San Francisco. The Marshall Plan for reconstruction of war-damaged locations adopted. Formation of NATO (North Atlantic Treaty Organization). 1950–1951—the Korean War ends in a truce in 1953.

1953–1961 DWIGHT D. EISENHOWER (Republican)

Hawaii and Alaska become states. *Brown v. Board of Education*. Southeast Asia Treaty Organization formed. Space exploration begins, *Sputnik 1* orbits the earth.

1961–1963 JOHN F. KENNEDY (Democrat)

Peace Corps established. Cuban missile crisis. United States guarantees South Vietnam protection from aggression. Nuclear test ban treaty ratified. President assassinated on November 22, 1963, to be succeeded by the vice president, Lyndon Johnson.

1963–1969 LYNDON B. JOHNSON (Democrat)

War on Poverty, the Economic Opportunity Act passed. The war in Vietnam supported with massive military and air aid. Medicare program established. President chooses to not run again.

1969–1974 RICHARD M. NIXON (Republican)

Massive protests against Vietnam war lead to some troops coming home. The president visits China. Astronauts land on the moon. The president is implicated in the Watergate scandal. Televised hearings in the Senate are held regarding a cover-up by the Nixon Administration. Vice President Spiro Agnew resigns; President Nixon appoints Gerald Ford, and his appointment is confirmed by the Senate. Shocking revelations about Watergate are made; the president resigns August 8, 1974, to be succeeded by the vice president, Gerald Ford.

1974–1977 GERALD R. FORD (Republican)

Nixon is granted "full, free and absolute pardon for any crimes he may have committed." President Ford visits South Korea and Japan.

1977–1981 JAMES E. (JIMMY) CARTER (Democrat)

Panama Canal Zone lease terminated. Middle East peace treaties drawn up. SALT II (Strategic Arms Limitation Treaty) negotiated with Russia. In Iran militant students occupy the U.S. embassy and hold 52 Americans hostage. Unsuccessful rescue efforts by the United States are abandoned; eight persons die and the remaining are cruelly treated. Carter is not reelected president, losing the election to Republican Ronald Reagan in a landslide. On the day that the new president is sworn in, January 20, 1981, the hostages are released in Teheran.

1981–1989 RONALD REAGAN (Republican)

Republicans control Senate for the first time in 30 years. First woman appointed to Supreme Court—Sandra Day O'Connor. Budget priorities: sharp increase in defense expenditures with decrease in social programs. 1984 Reagan wins reelection, again by a landslide. Summit meeting with Gorbachev in Geneva. Military aid to Contras in Nicaragua increased by financial help amounting to $100 million. Appointed to Supreme Court: William H. Rehnquist, Chief Justice; Antonin Scalia, Associate Justice. Space shuttle *Challenger* explodes, killing six astronauts, including first woman. Star Wars program encouraged. Huge trade deficit—a record $169.78 billion.

1989–1993 GEORGE H. W. BUSH (Republican)

Previously vice president to Ronald Reagan, End of Cold War; end of Soviet Union. Noriega overthrown in Panama. Operation Desert Storm successful in the Middle East.

1993–2001 WILLIAM JEFFERSON (BILL) CLINTON (Democrat)
Previously governor of Arkansas. Globalism, peace, and prosperity. Impeached by House of Representatives, but found not guilty when tried by the Senate.

2001–2009 GEORGE W. BUSH (Republican)
Son of President George H. W. Bush. Previously governor of Texas. Terrorist attack on World Trade Center and Pentagon on 9/11/2001. War on Terrorism, Congress appropriates funds to fight. Liberation of Afghanistan from Taliban. War with Iraq—capture of Saddam Hussein, who is later executed.

2009–   BARACK H. OBAMA (Democrat)
First African-American president. Former senator from Illinois. Passed Affordable Care Act in 2010. Death of Osama Bin Laden in 2011. Ended war in Iraq in 2011.

The Court System

The **judicial branch** of the government is responsible for interpreting the laws. The Constitution calls for one Supreme Court and "such inferior [lower] courts as the Congress shall from time to time ordain and establish." Congress has set up a series of lower federal courts that have the right to hear and decide cases under federal laws. This system of courts includes district courts, courts of appeal, and finally the **Supreme Court,** the highest court of the country. Once the Supreme Court has made a decision, that is the last word. There can be no further appeal.

There are nine judges on the Supreme Court, all appointed by the president for life. When a case comes before the Supreme Court, the justices hear it together. The decision is reached by majority vote. Sometimes, justices who disagree, or **dissent,** write minority or dissenting opinions. But the majority vote is final.

In 1981 the first woman justice, Sandra Day O'Connor, was appointed to the Supreme Court. Currently, three women sit on the Supreme Court: Ruth Bader Ginsburg, Sonia Sotomayor, and Elena Kagan. Sandra Day O'Connor retired in 2006.

The lower federal courts have jurisdiction, or authority, in disputes over government security, immigration, national banks, shipping on the high seas, and other matters. Cases that most of us are involved in are decided at the state or local level. Each state has a network of courts in which persons who have broken state laws are tried. Each city also has courts in which cases involving local laws are tried.

REVIEW

Do you know what these words mean? Write the meanings next to the words. If you are not sure, look up the meaning in the Word List in the Appendix.

1. appeal _____

2. dispute_____

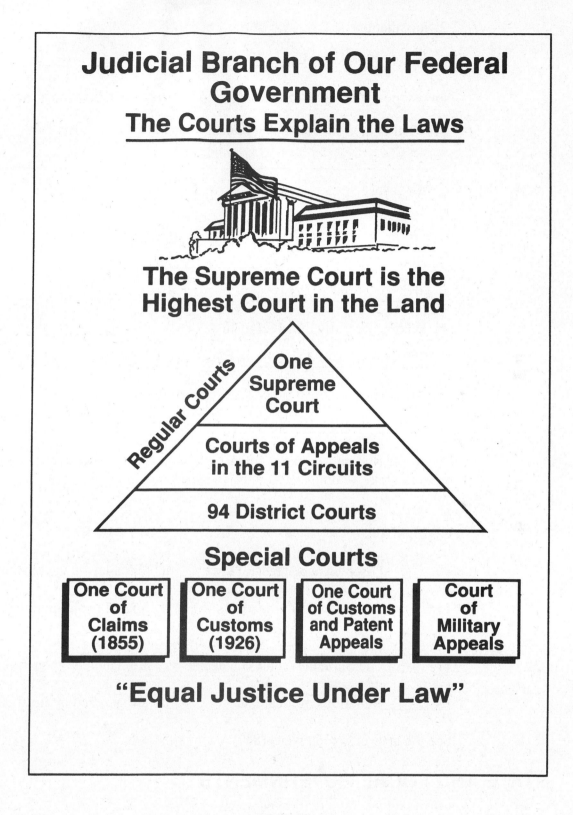

Judicial Branch of Our Federal Government
The Courts Explain the Laws

The Supreme Court is the Highest Court in the Land

Regular Courts

One Supreme Court

Courts of Appeals in the 11 Circuits

94 District Courts

Special Courts

| One Court of Claims (1855) | One Court of Customs (1926) | One Court of Customs and Patent Appeals | Court of Military Appeals |

"Equal Justice Under Law"

Figure 14

Source: U.S. Department of Justice, Immigration and Naturalization Service

3. jurisdiction _____

4. dissent (dissenting) _____

Now, write the answers to the following questions in the space provided.

5. What is the function of the judicial branch of the government? _____

_____

6. What is the highest court in the United States? _____

_____

7. How is this court set up? _____

_____

8. Who is presently the chief justice? _____

_____

9. Are there any courts other than federal courts? _____

_____

Match the first part of each sentence (column A) with the letter in column B in order to make a complete thought. (Choices may be repeated.)

COLUMN A

10. _____ Disputes under federal laws

11. _____ Naturalization procedures

12. _____ The Supreme Court can decide

13. _____ Violations of local law

COLUMN B

a. that a law is unconstitutional.

b. related to shipping on the high sea.

c. are handled by federal courts.

d. are handled by local courts.

See the answer key on page 183.

STATE AND LOCAL GOVERNMENTS

State Government

When you apply for naturalization, you must prove that you have lived for at least three months in the state from which you apply. You should know the names of the governor and the two senators from your state.

Each of the 50 states has three branches of government—legislative, executive, judicial—just like the U.S. federal government, but not all of them function in the same way. The reason that different patterns emerged is because the 13 original colonies had governments before the U.S. Constitution was ratified in 1789. The first to have its own constitution was New Hampshire. In fact, if you visit New Hampshire today, you will see the nation's oldest state legislature still functioning in its original chambers.

Like Congress, the state legislatures make laws for the state, but they cannot make laws that affect all Americans. They cannot declare war, regulate post offices, coin money, control trade with foreign countries, or decide who can become American citizens. According to the U.S. Constitution (the Tenth Amendment), the states have those powers that are not granted to the federal government and that are not specifically denied to them. This gives the states a great deal of power over our everyday lives. Education, health, sanitation, police and fire protection, and voting procedures are some examples of state functions. States impose taxes, even income taxes, regulate businesses that operate within their borders, and perform many functions that protect the lives and property of their residents.

Each state has a chief executive, or governor, elected by the people of the state, who makes sure that the laws are carried out. Like the president, the governor has people to assist and advise him.

The judicial branch of state governments includes a set of courts that have authority to try civil and criminal cases; some states have family and children's courts. All have courts of appeal. All states have correctional departments that regulate jails and prisons within their jurisdiction.

Local Government

Within the states there are smaller subdivisions—counties, cities, towns, and villages—that have governments, too. Laws for their residents are made by bodies often called councils, which have the authority to control streets, traffic, water supply, garbage, parking, and other everyday services. Cities and counties may also impose taxes, such as property and school taxes.

This government has an executive branch too, sometimes headed by a mayor or commissioner, which sees that local laws are enforced. And there is a judicial branch, consisting of municipal courts, traffic courts, and, in some cases, small claims courts. Local governments vary most from state to state. Find out how your local government functions, and when you become a citizen, get involved at this level! It is at this level that residents are in closest contact with their elected officials.

As you learn more about what state and local governments can do, remember that the U.S. Constitution is the supreme law of the land and the Supreme Court can find laws unconstitutional if they go against the Constitution.

HOW THE ORGANIZATION OF GOVERNMENT IN CITIES, STATES, AND THE NATION IS MUCH ALIKE

	Each has a legislative branch to make laws	Each has an executive branch to enforce the laws	Each has a judicial branch to explain and apply the laws
The Federal Government:	The Congress—Senate and House of Representatives.	President, vice president, 15 executive departments, and other executive agencies.	The federal courts.
The State Government:	The state legislature. (Two houses in all states but Nebraska.)	The governor and heads of executive departments.	The state courts.
The City Government:	The city council or commissioners.	The mayor or manager or board of commissioners.	The city courts.

Figure 15

Source: U.S. Department of Justice, Immigration and Naturalization Service

DELEGATED POWERS IN THE FEDERAL SYSTEM

A. POWERS OF THE FEDERAL GOVERNMENT
(those DELEGATED to it)

EXAMPLES

To control relations with foreign nations.

To punish crimes against the United States.

To establish post offices.

To coin money and regulate its value.

To keep up an army, a navy, and an air corps.

To declare war and make peace.

To set standards for weights and measures.

To regulate commerce among the States and with foreign countries.

To make uniform laws about naturalization and bankruptcy.

To protect authors and inventors by giving copyrights and patents.

To admit new States and to control the territory of the United States.

To make all laws necessary and proper for carrying into effect the expressly stated powers and all other powers granted by the United States Constitution.

B. CONCURRENT POWERS*

EXAMPLES

To borrow money.

To collect taxes.

To build public works.

To charter banks.

To establish courts.

To help agriculture and industry.

To protect the public health.

C. PROHIBITED POWERS

EXAMPLES

To deny civil rights (such as freedom of speech, press, religion, and assembly).

To pass laws that make illegal something that has already been done legally and honestly.

To pass a law that finds any person guilty without trial.

D. POWERS OF THE STATES (called RESERVED powers)

EXAMPLES

To authorize the establishment of local governments.

To establish and keep up schools.

To regulate city government groups.

To provide for a state militia.

To regulate commerce within the borders of the state.

To regulate labor, industry, and business within the state.

To provide care for orphans and paupers, and for blind, crippled, insane, and other helpless persons.

To make laws on all other subjects not prohibited to the states by the federal or state constitutions, and not delegated to the federal government.

*Concurrent means belonging to both federal and state governments.

Figure 16

Source: U.S. Department of Justice, Immigration and Naturalization Service

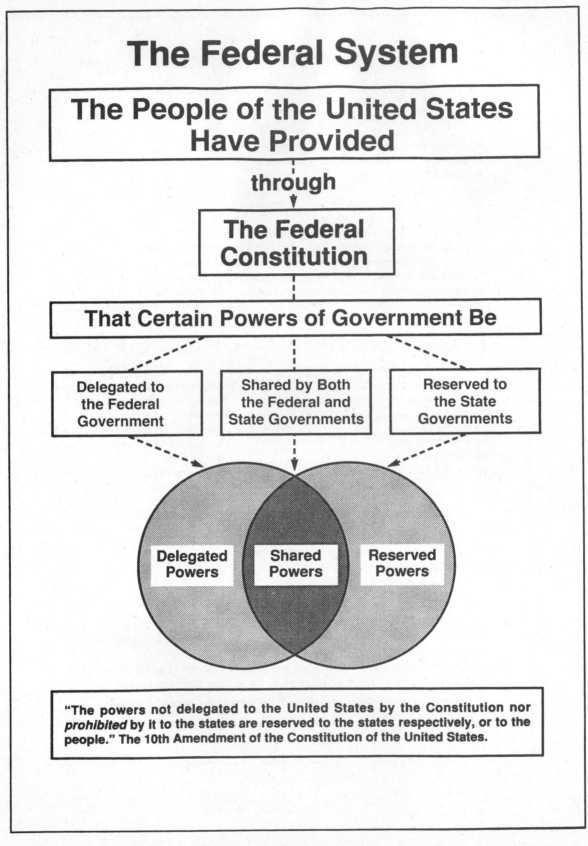

The Federal System

The People of the United States Have Provided

through

The Federal Constitution

That Certain Powers of Government Be

| Delegated to the Federal Government | Shared by Both the Federal and State Governments | Reserved to the State Governments |

Delegated Powers   **Shared Powers**   **Reserved Powers**

"**The powers not delegated to the United States by the Constitution nor** *prohibited* **by it to the states are reserved to the states respectively, or to the people.**" **The 10th Amendment of the Constitution of the United States.**

Figure 17

Source: U.S. Department of Justice, Immigration and Naturalization Service

REVIEW

Do you know what these words mean? Write the meanings next to the words. If you are not sure, look up the meaning in the Word List in the Appendix.

1. function _____

2. executive _____

3. ratify _____

4. legislative _____

5. legislature _____

6. judicial _____

7. jurisdiction _____

8. unconstitutional _____

Now, write the answer to the following question in the space provided.

9. How does the U.S. Constitution grant rights to the 50 states?_____

_____

See the answer key on page 183.

THE AMERICAN FLAG

The **flag** is a symbol of our country. The colors of the flag have special meanings: RED is for courage; WHITE is for truth; BLUE is for honor. The American national **anthem** is the **"Star-Spangled Banner,"** which refers to the flag. Sometimes the flag is called other names—Old Glory; the Stars and Stripes; the Red, White, and Blue; or just the Colors. Before the American Revolution, most of the colonies used the British flag. But when anger grew at their treatment by Great Britain, the colonists took down that flag and put up their own.

One year after the Declaration of Independence, in 1777, the American flag was officially adopted. It was made by Betsy Ross. The first flag had 13 stripes, to mark the colonies, and 13 stars, to mark the 13 states. There are still the same number of stripes as in 1777; the number of stars, however, has changed as new states joined the union. The flag that was flown on the moon when the American astronauts landed there in 1969 had 50 stars and 13 stripes. It is the same today. Flag Day is June 14, for it was on that day in 1777 that the first American flag was adopted.

Have you gone to any public meetings where the Pledge of Allegiance was said? You will remember that people stood up and placed their right hands over their hearts as they said these words:

PLEDGE OF ALLEGIANCE

I pledge allegiance to the flag of the United States of America and to the Republic for which it stands, one nation under God, indivisible, with liberty and justice for all.

Where did you hear the word *allegiance* before? That's right! In the final step in the naturalization process, before becoming an American citizen, you must take the Oath of Allegiance. Let's read it.

OATH OF ALLEGIANCE

I hereby declare, on oath, that I absolutely and entirely renounce and abjure all allegiance and fidelity to any foreign prince, potentate, state, or sovereignty, of whom or which I have heretofore been a subject or citizen; that I will support and defend the Constitution and laws of the United States of America against all enemies, foreign and domestic; that I will bear true faith and allegiance to the same; that I will bear arms on behalf of the United States when required by the law; that I will perform noncombatant service in the Armed Forces of the United States when required by the law; that I will perform work of national importance under civilian direction when required by the law; and that I take this obligation freely without any mental reservation or purpose of evasion; so help me God.

REVIEW

Do you know what these words mean? Write the meanings next to the words. If you are not sure, look up the meaning in the Word List in the Appendix.

1. symbol _____

2. anthem _____

3. "Star-Spangled Banner" _____

4. adopted _____

5. Pledge of Allegiance _____

Now, complete the following sentences in the space provided by adding the word *because* and giving a reason.

Example: We show respect to the flag *because it is the symbol of our country.*

6. The flag is sometimes called the Red, White, and Blue _____

_____

7. The flag has 13 stripes _____

_____

8. It has 50 stars _____

_____

9. Before the American Revolution, most of the colonies used the British flag

_____

10. June 14 is celebrated as Flag Day _____

_____

See the answer key on page 183.

DISPLAYING THE FLAG

Here are two things that we should know about the use of the American flag:

1. When we display the American flag with other flags, our flag should always have the place of honor.
2. The American flag should not be used in advertising (sales, and so on).

A GLIMPSE AT AMERICAN HISTORY

THE EARLY YEARS—EXPLORING AND SETTLING A NEW LAND

What is now the United States began with the "discovery" of America by Christopher Columbus on October 12, 1492. Spanish settlements in the New World followed. (Columbus Day is a legal holiday today.) In the 17th and early 18th centuries, the Dutch, the Swedes, the Germans, and the French established settlements here. The British made the largest permanent settlements. The settlers came primarily for religious and political freedom and to escape persecution in their native lands. The first English colony was at Jamestown (Virginia) in 1607.

The largest settlement came soon after in 1620, when the group we call the Pilgrims—about 100 men and women—sailed from England on the *Mayflower*. They came for religious freedom, and, after landing on the coast of what is now Massachusetts, they wrote and signed an agreement, the Mayflower Compact, that promised to make laws for the good of all settlers. This was the first written constitution in the New World.

Pilgrims Signing the Mayflower Compact, 1620

(Source: Library of Congress)

American Indians (Native Americans) lived in America before any Europeans arrived. The Indians helped the Pilgrims survive in their new world. They showed the settlers how to grow native crops such as corn and squash. With the Indians' help, the Pilgrims grew enough food to survive the winter. The Pilgrims held a Thanksgiving feast in 1621 to celebrate the successful harvest. This Thanksgiving feast was the first holiday celebrated by American colonists, and it is a traditional holiday today.

With the expansion of their lands, the settlers needed help. They brought in Africans to work as slaves on their plantations.

THE ERA OF THE AMERICAN REVOLUTION AND INDEPENDENCE

By the middle of the 18th century, there were 13 colonies along the East Coast of the new land. Although some people came from other countries, these colonies were considered dependent on England as their "mother country." They were often referred to as the 13 English colonies and were required to pay taxes to England. Colonists found it hard to pay taxes as they became higher and higher. Some colonists believed that taxation without representation was wrong. They protested, and England sent troops to enforce the laws. That was the beginning of the War for Independence—the American Revolution.

SOME OF OUR FIRST IMMIGRANTS

People from many foreign lands came and settled in this new world. They sought liberty and a better living, and the happiness they hoped these would bring them. Here are some of the early arrivals:

1565	The SPANISH settled at St. Augustine, in what is now Florida.
1607	The ENGLISH settled at Jamestown, in what is now Virginia.
1620	The ENGLISH (Pilgrims) settled in what is now Massachusetts.
1623–1625	The DUTCH settled on Manhattan Island, where New York City has since been built.
1638	The SWEDES settled in what is now the State of Delaware.
1681	The ENGLISH (Quakers) settled in what is now Pennsylvania.
1683	The GERMANS settled at Germantown and other places in Pennsylvania.
1714	The SCOTTISH and IRISH settled in large numbers along the western edge of all the colonies from Pennsylvania to Georgia.
1718	The FRENCH settled in New Orleans, at the mouth of the Mississippi River.

Figure 18

Source: U.S. Department of Justice, Immigration and Naturalization Service

**The Protest Against British Taxes, Known as the
"Boston Tea Party," 1773**

(Source: Library of Congress)

Some of the great leaders of that time were George Washington, Thomas Jefferson, and Patrick Henry. These leaders believed that if a government is not protecting the rights of its people, the people can take away the power of the government. So the colonists took back their power and declared independence from Great Britain. Patrick Henry, one of the great patriots and orators of the time, helped push the colonies toward independence when he said, "Give me liberty or give me death."

The 4th of July—Independence Day—is our most important national holiday. It is the date of our official Declaration of Independence from Great Britain, and it is considered to be the birthday of America. Thomas Jefferson—who later became the third president of the United States—was the main writer of the Declaration of Independence. A copy of the Declaration of Independence, including signatures of the delegates, is in this book. Look at it now. Some of the ideas in the Declaration of Independence are that all men are created equal and have the right to life, liberty, and the pursuit of happiness.

By 1787, a document that described the role the central government should have in the new country was clearly needed. A Constitutional Convention was convened to write the Constitution. George Washington, the military commander who had led our country to victory during the American Revolution, was chosen to be the leader of the convention. The oldest delegate to the convention was Benjamin Franklin. Franklin had been an inventor, a writer (*Poor Richard's Almanac*), and a diplomat.

A main point of debate at the convention was how much power the federal government would have and how much power would be left to the states. Delegates who favored a strong central government were called Federalists. Delegates who favored states' rights were called anti-Federalists. The Federalists (including Alexander Hamilton, James Madison, and John Jay) published 85 newspaper articles, signed with the name "Publius." These articles, which are called the *Federalist Papers*, tried to get readers to support the passage of the Constitution.

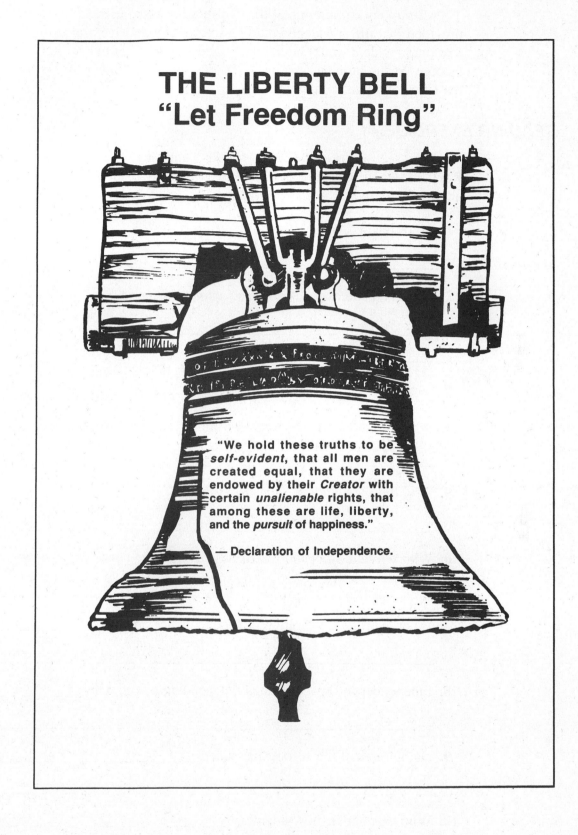

Figure 19

Source: U.S. Department of Justice, Immigration and Naturalization Service

After many compromises, the Constitution was ratified (approved). It provided that the president would be selected by an Electoral College, and also that the president would be the commander-in-chief of our military forces. George Washington became our first president (the "father of our country") and the first commander-in-chief.

READING EXERCISE #1

Read the sections titled "The Early Years" and "The Era of the American Revolution and Independence" and answer each question below. Check your answers with the answer key on pages 183–184.

1. Who lived in America before the Europeans arrived? _____

   _____

2. What is one reason the colonists came to America? _____

   _____

3. Who helped the Pilgrims in America? _____

   _____

4. What holiday was celebrated for the first time by American colonists? _____

   _____

5. Why did the colonists fight the British? _____

   _____

6. Who wrote the Declaration of Independence?_____

   _____

7. When was the Declaration of Independence adopted? _____

   _____

8. Independence Day celebrates independence from whom?_____

   _____

9. Name three of the 13 original states. _____

   _____

10. Who was our first president? _____

   _____

11. Who is the "father of our country"?_____

_____

12. What happened at the Constitutional Convention? _____

_____

13. When was the Constitution written? _____

_____

14. Name one of the writers of the *Federalist Papers*._____

_____

15. Name one thing Benjamin Franklin is famous for. _____

_____

THE 1800s

• <u>Westward Expansion</u>

Take a look at the territorial acquisition map. Both peace and war faced the new nation as it grew. In some cases, the United States bought new territory. In 1803, for example, we bought territory from France (the Louisiana Purchase) for about $15 million. This purchase doubled the size of the United States.

In some cases, settlers were protected, and land was acquired in battles. As the settlers moved west, they faced attacks from American Indian tribes who wanted to maintain their own culture. The British encouraged these attacks. This was one of the causes of another war with England—the War of 1812. The war ended in 1814. Both the British and the Americans returned the land they had captured, and a commission (an official group) was set up to determine the border between the United States and Canada.

In 1836, Texas became independent from Mexico. In 1845, it requested annexation by the United States. In December of 1845, it became our 28th state. However, Mexico disputed its southern boundary, and the Mexican-American War broke out. A primary cause of the war was the desire of the pro-slavery party in the United States to expand the slave territory. And President Polk wanted to gain for the new nation all of the Texas, New Mexico, California, and Oregon territories. The Mexican-American War ended in 1848, with the ceding of the New Mexico and California territories to the United States. The Oregon territory was added to the United States in 1846 after an agreement with the British that established its boundary.

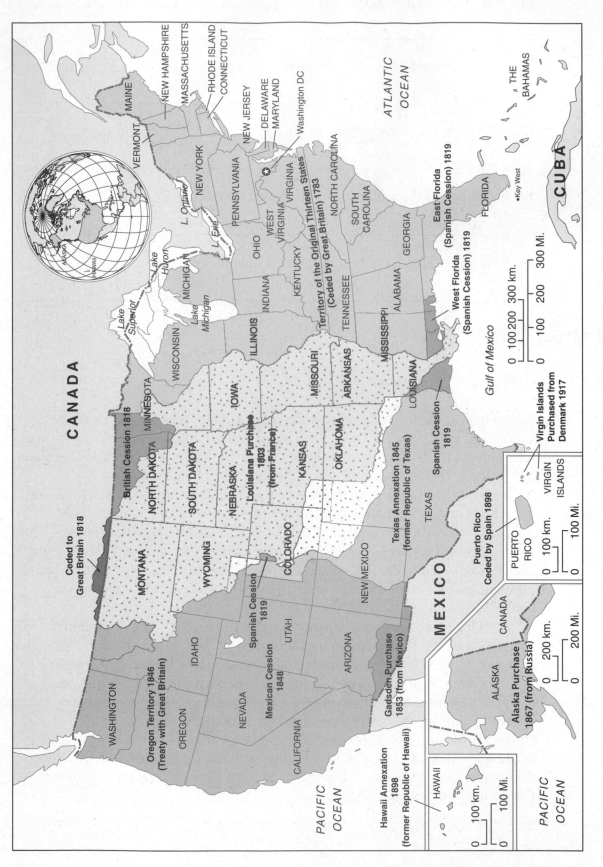

The United States of America—Territorial Acquisitions

• <u>Abraham Lincoln, the Civil War, and the Emancipation Proclamation</u>

Abraham Lincoln was born into a very poor family, but he later became one of the most important presidents of the United States. In 1860, he was elected to become the 16th president of the United States, mainly because of his opposition to slavery. By that time, most northern states had abolished slavery, but the agricultural states in the South still wanted slaves to work on their plantations. After Lincoln's election, southern states began to secede (break away) from the United States. They based their secession on a doctrine called "states' rights," which gives citizens of individual states the power to nullify (overturn) federal laws.

After Lincoln's inauguration in 1861, he urged all sections of the United States (the Union) to remain united. He used all his powers to avoid a civil war, but his efforts failed. On April 12, 1861, the war began with the bombardment of a Union fort, Fort Sumter, South Carolina.

President Abraham Lincoln (center) at a Union
Army Encampment, October 1862

(Source: Library of Congress)

By the middle of the Civil War, President Lincoln concluded that the nation could never exist as half-slave and half-free. He issued the Emancipation Proclamation, which freed the slaves in the Confederate states. In 1865, the Union (northern) soldiers defeated the Confederate (southern) soldiers and the war ended on April 9, 1865.

• The Reconstruction Period

Upon the assassination of Abraham Lincoln on April 15, 1865, the vice president, Andrew Johnson, became the president of the United States. Following Lincoln's plan, he readmitted the Confederate states to the Union after they ratified the Thirteenth Amendment abolishing slavery. Decoration Day (now called Memorial Day) was set up to honor the fallen of the war. After a series of conflicts, Johnson was impeached by the House of Representatives, but the Senate found him not guilty by one vote.

• American Indians (Native Americans)

With the westward expansion of the country, most American Indian tribes were compelled to move farther and farther west, often by force. The Indians were generally moved onto reservations (lands set aside for the tribes) or totally obliterated (wiped out). Conflicts with the settlers, disease, displacement, and enslavement resulted in a decline in their population from about 1 million before the arrival of the Europeans to about 250,000 by the end of the 19th century.

A Wichita Camp
Photo by Henry Peabody, ca. 1904

(Source: The National Archives)

During the early 20th century, there were some improvements in the lives of the Indians (although reservations continue to exist). By 1924, about two-thirds of the Indians had already been granted American citizenship, and the Citizenship Act of 1924 extended citizenship to all Indians born in the United States. Currently there are 561 federally recognized tribes in the United States, including Navajo, Cherokee, Choctaw, Sioux, Seminole, Chippewa, Blackfeet, Apache, Mohegan, Oneida, Iroquois, and Pueblo.

• <u>**Women's Suffrage**</u>

**Suffragists March on Pennsylvania Avenue,
Washington, D.C., 1913**

(Source: Library of Congress)

With the passage of the Fifteenth Amendment, all **men**, including former slaves, were free to vote. However, **women** still were not allowed to vote or hold public office. In 1848, the first women's suffrage convention was held in Seneca Falls, New York. (*Suffrage* means "the right to vote.") Some of the leaders of the women's suffrage movement were Elizabeth Cady Stanton and Susan B. Anthony. These women and their organizations worked tirelessly for women's rights, and in 1919 a women's suffrage amendment passed both houses of Congress. In 1920, the Nineteenth Amendment was ratified by the states.

• <u>**The Spanish-American War**</u>

In 1898, concerns about the treatment of Spanish subjects in Cuba led the United States to send the battleship *Maine* into Havana Harbor to protect American interests. The *Maine* was blown up, and the United States declared war on Spain. The war ended in 1899. Spain gave up its claims to Cuba and ceded Puerto Rico, the Philippines, and Guam to the United States for $20 million. Theodore Roosevelt became well-known as the commander of the Rough Riders and, on his return home, was elected governor of New York and later president of the United States.

READING EXERCISE #2

Read the paragraphs about the 1800s and answer the following questions. Check your answers with the answer key on page 184.

1. What territory did the United States buy from France in 1803? _____
_____

2. Name one war fought by the United States in the 1800s. _____
_____

3. Name the U.S. war between the North and the South. _____
_____

4. Name *one* problem that led to the Civil War. _____
_____

5. What was *one* important thing that Abraham Lincoln did? _____
_____

6. What did the Emancipation Proclamation do? _____
_____

7. Name *one* American Indian tribe in the United States. _____
_____

8. What did Susan B. Anthony do? _____
_____

RECENT AMERICAN HISTORY

• World War I (1914–1918)

World War I began in Europe in 1914. In 1917, President Woodrow Wilson broke off diplomatic relations with Germany when German submarines made the seas unsafe for American vessels. He requested Congress to declare war on Germany, and Congress approved. During World War I, the draft (conscription) of men between the ages of 21 and 30 was instituted.

Germany surrendered on November 11, 1918, and Veterans' Day, November 11, is a federal holiday.

• <u>The Great Depression (1930s)</u>

Following the stock market crash on October 29, 1929, banks failed, factories closed, and workers lost their jobs. Many people lost their savings and their homes. The president, Herbert Hoover, refused to provide government services to help the people, many of whom were close to starvation. In the 1932 election, Franklin Roosevelt defeated Hoover by a landslide. Roosevelt promised a "New Deal," to turn the economy around. With the support of Congress, he created programs to provide jobs and other programs, such as Social Security, to provide "safety nets." The Depression ended with the start of World War II, when factories began hiring workers again.

• <u>World War II (1938–1945)</u>

Battleships USS *West Virginia* and USS *Tennessee* After the Japanese Attack on Pearl Harbor, December 7, 1941

(Source: The National Archives)

Again the war began in Europe. On December 7, 1941, Japan entered the war by declaring war on the United States and Great Britain and then attacking the U.S. naval fleet at Pearl Harbor in Hawaii. President Roosevelt asked Congress to declare war on Japan, and on December 11, 1941, Congress approved the war. Hitler (Germany) and Mussolini (Italy) then declared war on the United States, and Congress responded by declaring war on those two countries. Dwight D. Eisenhower, who later became the 34th president of the United States, was the supreme commander of Allied forces in Europe. The war in Europe ended with Germany's unconditional surrender on May 7, 1945.

The war in the Pacific continued, however. On August 6, 1945, President Truman (who became president after the death of President Roosevelt in April 1945) authorized the use of the first atomic bomb, which was dropped on Hiroshima, Japan. It caused unbelievable destruction, and on August 10, 1945, Japan asked for peace. Japan surrendered unconditionally on September 2, 1945.

• The United Nations (U.N.)

The Flag of the United Nations

The United Nations was established in 1945 shortly after the end of World War II. The Charter of the U.N. provides ways in which nations of the world may work toward cooperative solutions of international problems. The two best-known parts of the U.N. are the General Assembly, which is made up of more than 190 countries, and the Security Council, which is made up of 10 countries. The United States is one of the five permanent members of the Security Council.

• The Cold War

The Cold War was a period of intense military and technological competition between the United States and the Soviet Union following World War II. The main concern of the United States during the Cold War was preventing the spread of communism. The Cold War ended with the fall of the Berlin Wall in 1989.

• The Civil Rights Movement

Although slaves were freed during the Civil War and all men—not just white men—were given the right to vote by the Fifteenth Amendment, life in the United States continued to be segregated (separated by race) into the 20th century. In fact, "separate but equal" was the law of the land. This meant, especially in the South, that black children were not allowed to go to schools reserved for white children. Black people had to ride at the back of bus, and they couldn't use the same restrooms and water fountains as white people.

In the 1950s, black people began demanding a change. This was the start of the *civil rights movement*. One of the great leaders of the movement was Dr. Martin Luther King, Jr. Dr. King believed in using nonviolent methods, such as boycotts, to end segregation. His methods resulted in great changes, but the reaction to the movement became more and more violent. In April 1968, Dr. King was assassinated in Memphis, Tennessee.

• Rivers and Lakes

The two longest rivers in the United States are the Mississippi and the Missouri. The Mississippi River flows south from Minnesota to the Gulf of Mexico. The Missouri River flows from its source in Montana through North Dakota and South Dakota. Then it forms the border between the states of Nebraska and Iowa and Missouri. Finally it joins the Mississippi River north of St. Louis, Missouri.

The largest lakes in the United States are the five Great Lakes. Their names are Lakes Ontario, Erie, Huron, Michigan, and Superior. Except for Lake Michigan, which is completely within the United States, these lakes are part of the border between the United States and Canada.

• National Monuments and National Parks

National monuments and parks are public lands that have been set aside to preserve historic sites and wilderness areas for the enjoyment of all the people.

National monuments usually protect one unique resource, including historic landmarks, historic and prehistoric structures, and other objects of scientific interest. Some national monuments are the Grand Canyon in Arizona, the Little Bighorn Battlefield in Montana, and the African Burial Ground in New York City.

For immigrants and visitors to the United States, probably the best-known national monument is the Statue of Liberty on Liberty Island in New York harbor, between the states of New York and New Jersey. The people of France presented the statue to the United States to commemorate the 100th anniversary of the American Revolution. To most people, the statue is a symbol of freedom and escape from oppression.

Statue of Liberty

(Library of Congress)

• Other Major Events

- **The Vietnam War.** Beginning in the 1950s, the United States started providing military advisers to South Vietnam. We feared that the defeat of South Vietnam by communist North Vietnam would have a "domino effect," which would cause nearby countries also to fall to communism. Eventually the United States had more than 500,000 troops in Vietnam. In 1975, the last Americans were evacuated from Saigon (the capital of South Vietnam); communist forces took over the city. From 1959 to 1975, 58,000 Americans died in Vietnam.

- **The Persian Gulf War and the War in Iraq.** In August 1990, Iraqi dictator Saddam Hussein ordered his army to invade neighboring Kuwait. With the approval of the United Nations, the United States led a coalition of nations in Operation Desert Storm, an air war followed by a war on the ground. After 42 days, Saddam ordered his troops to leave Kuwait, and the Persian Gulf War was over. In 2003, the United States led a much smaller coalition in a second war in Iraq. American intelligence suggested that Iraq, under Saddam Hussein, was developing weapons of mass destruction and also that Iraq was supporting terrorists. Saddam was executed in December 2006. The war in Iraq ended in 2011.

- **September 11, 2001.** On that date, terrorists attacked two locations in the United States—the World Trade Center in New York and the Pentagon in Arlington, Virginia. The United States and its allies sent troops into Afghanistan, where the terrorists are believed to have their headquarters and training camps.

READING EXERCISE #3

Read the paragraphs about recent American history and answer the following questions. Check your answers with the answer key on page 184.

1. Name *one* war fought by the United States in the 1900s. _____

_____

2. Who was president during World War I? _____

_____

3. Who was president during the Great Depression and World War II? _____

_____

4. What countries did the United States fight in World War II? _____

_____

5. Before he was president, Eisenhower was a general. What war was he in? __

_____

6. During the Cold War, what was the main concern of the United States? ____

_____

7. What movement tried to end racial discrimination? _____

_____

8. What did Martin Luther King, Jr., do?_____

_____

9. What major event happened on September 11, 2001?_____

_____

A GLIMPSE AT GEOGRAPHY

Take a look at the states and capitals map. The United States of America is on the continent of North America, and its neighbors are Canada to the north and Mexico to the south.

• States and Territories

The map shows that we have 48 contiguous (adjoining) states and 2 non-contiguous states (Alaska and Hawaii). Alaska is the farthest north of our states. It borders on Canada, and is across the Bering Sea from Russia. Hawaii is our southernmost state. It is made up of a group of islands in the Pacific Ocean. Besides these 50 states, there is the District of Columbia, where our nation's capital, Washington, D.C., is located. Look for the District of Columbia on the map. You'll find it on the east coast of the United States, between the states of Maryland and Virginia.

The United States also has five territories: Puerto Rico, U.S. Virgin Islands, American Samoa, Northern Mariana Islands, and Guam. (In most cases, people born in Puerto Rico, the U.S. Virgin Islands, the Northern Mariana Islands, and Guam are automatically citizens of the United States.)

• Mountain Ranges

There are three major mountain ranges in the United States. The longest and highest are the Rocky Mountains, which extend from New Mexico to Alaska. The Coastal Range is on the west coast; it extends from California through Oregon and Washington to Canada. The Appalachian Mountains are in the eastern United States. They extend from Alabama to Canada.

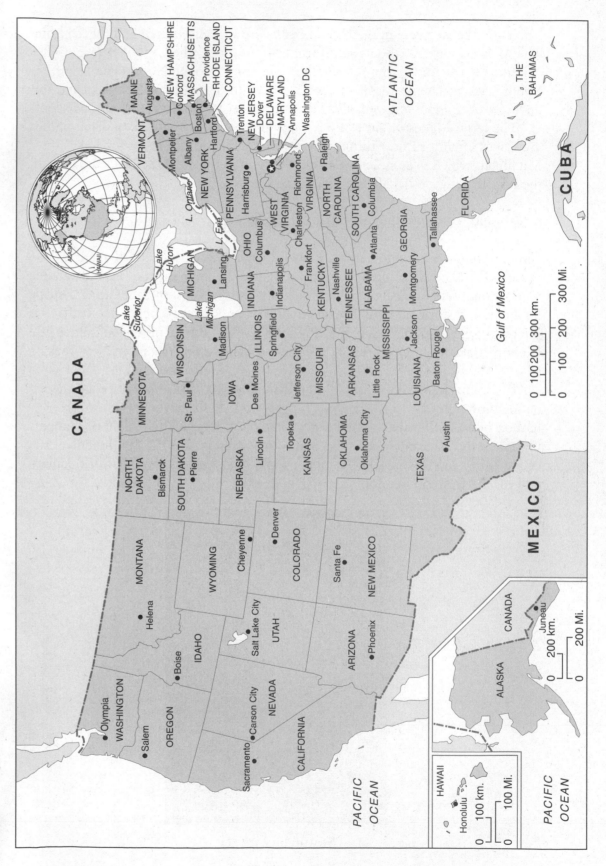

The United States of America—States and Capitals

National parks are usually much larger than national monuments. Their purpose includes the preservation of scenery and wildlife. Some well-known national parks are Yosemite National Park in California; Yellowstone National Park in Idaho, Montana, and Wyoming; and Denali National Park in Alaska.

READING EXERCISE

Read the paragraphs about the geography of the United States. From the information on the map and in the paragraphs, answer the following questions. Check your answers with the answer key on page 185.

1. What does the word *contiguous* mean? _____

    _____

2. What ocean is on the west coast of the United States? _____

    _____

3. What ocean is on the east coast of the United States? _____

    _____

4. The longest and highest mountain range in the United States is the _____.

    _____

5. Two states that are on the Canadian border are _____ and _____.

6. Two states on our border with Mexico are _____ and _____.

7. The two longest rivers in the United States are _____ and _____.

8. _____ is the nation's capital.

9. The names of the Great Lakes are _____, _____,

    _____, _____, and _____.

10. The largest of the Great Lakes is _____.

11. Two of the five territories of the United States are _____ and

    _____.

12. Where is the Statue of Liberty? _____

APPENDIX
FOR READY REFERENCE

Word List

A abbreviation................................a shortened form of a word

ability...knowledge and skill needed to do something

abolished ....put an end to; did away with

abridge.......................................to make shorter; to lessen

accept...to receive

active ....moving; doing one's work, doing things

adjourn ....to put off to a later time

administer...................................to direct or to give

admitted......................................given the right to enter

adopted ....accepted; agreed to; taken as one's own

adult..full-grown; matured

advantage....................................benefit

advise..inform; tell

afford ....to be able to spend money for something

agency...a company or office or organization in business to act for another's benefit

agree ....to say "yes"; to have the same opinion

agriculture ....the science of farming land

alien...a person from a foreign country; person not yet a citizen

amnesty ....a pardon

allegiance.....................................loyalty

allow ....to permit

amendment ....a change or an addition to a constitution or law

amount..the total sum

annexation ....uniting; adding to

anthem ....a song or hymn of praise or allegiance

appeal ....to take a question from a lower to a higher authority

appeared ....was seen; seemed to be

applicant ....a person who applies for something

application ....a form used to make a request

apply ....to ask for something; to let people know you want something

appointed ....named to take a job or office

apportion ....to make a division

approve ....to agree to; to think well of; to say "yes"

area ....amount of land; level space

WORD	MEANING
argue	to discuss; to give reasons in support of ideas
arrive	to reach a place; to come
assassinate	to kill or murder suddenly
assemble	to meet together for a common purpose
assistance	help; aid
attorney	a person acting for another person at law
avoid	to keep away from

B

WORD	MEANING
backbone	the most important part
background	the result of training, experience, education
balance	to make equal in value; to make even
base	foundation
basic	serving as a starting point
basis	the main part; supporting element
belief	faith; trust
belongings	things a person owns
benefit	anything that is for the good of a person or thing; money paid to a person
bill	a suggested law proposed by a lawmaker
Bill of Rights	the first ten amendments to the Constitution
borrow	to get something from another person with the understanding that it must be returned
boundary	the line, real or imaginary, that shows where a piece of land ends
brief	short

C

WORD	MEANING
Cabinet	a group of advisers to the president
candidate	a person who runs for office
capital	the city where the government is located
Capitol	the building in which the U.S. Congress meets
cattle	farm animals; livestock
cause	the thing a person fights for; reason
cede	to turn over land usually by treaty
celebrate	to recognize and honor, as a holiday
census	an official count of people
center	a middle point; place where people meet
certificate	a written statement of proof of some fact
character (good)	a good name or a reputation for being responsible and moral
charge	to ask as a price; fee
cheaper	costing less
check	to control; to hold back; to restrain
chief executive	the highest officer of government
choice	a thing preferred; selection
choose	to decide to take; to pick out
circular	a printed paper containing information

- **Other Major Events**

  - **The Vietnam War.** Beginning in the 1950s, the United States started providing military advisers to South Vietnam. We feared that the defeat of South Vietnam by communist North Vietnam would have a "domino effect," which would cause nearby countries also to fall to communism. Eventually the United States had more than 500,000 troops in Vietnam. In 1975, the last Americans were evacuated from Saigon (the capital of South Vietnam); communist forces took over the city. From 1959 to 1975, 58,000 Americans died in Vietnam.

  - **The Persian Gulf War and the War in Iraq.** In August 1990, Iraqi dictator Saddam Hussein ordered his army to invade neighboring Kuwait. With the approval of the United Nations, the United States led a coalition of nations in Operation Desert Storm, an air war followed by a war on the ground. After 42 days, Saddam ordered his troops to leave Kuwait, and the Persian Gulf War was over. In 2003, the United States led a much smaller coalition in a second war in Iraq. American intelligence suggested that Iraq, under Saddam Hussein, was developing weapons of mass destruction and also that Iraq was supporting terrorists. Saddam was executed in December 2006. The war in Iraq ended in 2011.

  - **September 11, 2001.** On that date, terrorists attacked two locations in the United States—the World Trade Center in New York and the Pentagon in Arlington, Virginia. The United States and its allies sent troops into Afghanistan, where the terrorists are believed to have their headquarters and training camps.

READING EXERCISE #3

Read the paragraphs about recent American history and answer the following questions. Check your answers with the answer key on page 184.

1. Name *one* war fought by the United States in the 1900s. _____

_____

2. Who was president during World War I? _____

_____

3. Who was president during the Great Depression and World War II? _____

_____

4. What countries did the United States fight in World War II? _____

_____

5. Before he was president, Eisenhower was a general. What war was he in? __

_____

6. During the Cold War, what was the main concern of the United States? ____

_____

7. What movement tried to end racial discrimination? _____

_____

8. What did Martin Luther King, Jr., do?_____

_____

9. What major event happened on September 11, 2001?_____

_____

A GLIMPSE AT GEOGRAPHY

Take a look at the states and capitals map. The United States of America is on the continent of North America, and its neighbors are Canada to the north and Mexico to the south.

• <u>States and Territories</u>

The map shows that we have 48 contiguous (adjoining) states and 2 non-contiguous states (Alaska and Hawaii). Alaska is the farthest north of our states. It borders on Canada, and is across the Bering Sea from Russia. Hawaii is our southernmost state. It is made up of a group of islands in the Pacific Ocean. Besides these 50 states, there is the District of Columbia, where our nation's capital, Washington, D.C., is located. Look for the District of Columbia on the map. You'll find it on the east coast of the United States, between the states of Maryland and Virginia.

The United States also has five territories: Puerto Rico, U.S. Virgin Islands, American Samoa, Northern Mariana Islands, and Guam. (In most cases, people born in Puerto Rico, the U.S. Virgin Islands, the Northern Mariana Islands, and Guam are automatically citizens of the United States.)

• <u>Mountain Ranges</u>

There are three major mountain ranges in the United States. The longest and highest are the Rocky Mountains, which extend from New Mexico to Alaska. The Coastal Range is on the west coast; it extends from California through Oregon and Washington to Canada. The Appalachian Mountains are in the eastern United States. They extend from Alabama to Canada.

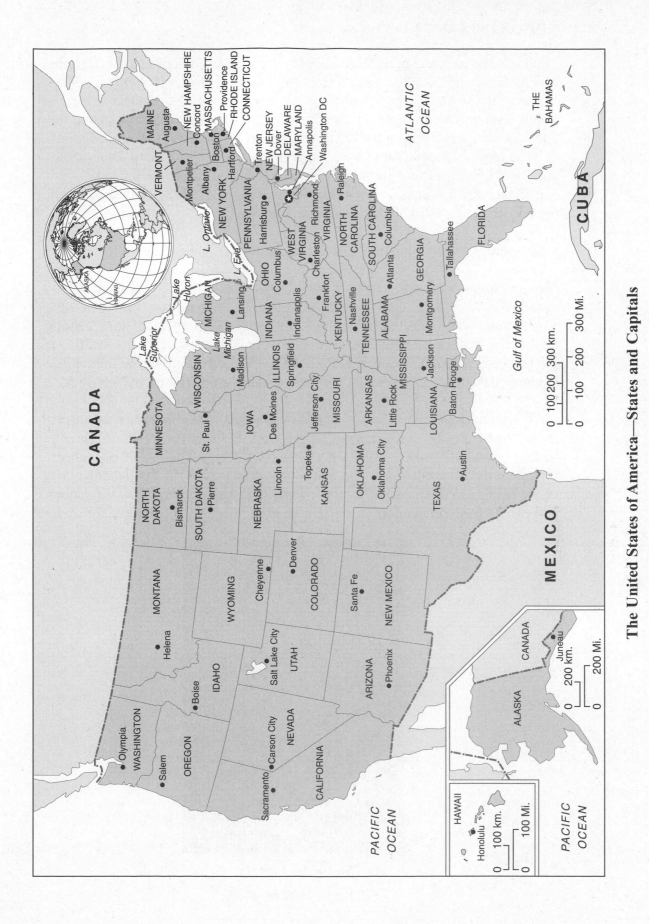

The United States of America—States and Capitals

• <u>Rivers and Lakes</u>

The two longest rivers in the United States are the Mississippi and the Missouri. The Mississippi River flows south from Minnesota to the Gulf of Mexico. The Missouri River flows from its source in Montana through North Dakota and South Dakota. Then it forms the border between the states of Nebraska and Iowa and Missouri. Finally it joins the Mississippi River north of St. Louis, Missouri.

The largest lakes in the United States are the five Great Lakes. Their names are Lakes Ontario, Erie, Huron, Michigan, and Superior. Except for Lake Michigan, which is completely within the United States, these lakes are part of the border between the United States and Canada.

• <u>National Monuments and National Parks</u>

National monuments and parks are public lands that have been set aside to preserve historic sites and wilderness areas for the enjoyment of all the people.

National monuments usually protect one unique resource, including historic landmarks, historic and prehistoric structures, and other objects of scientific interest. Some national monuments are the Grand Canyon in Arizona, the Little Bighorn Battlefield in Montana, and the African Burial Ground in New York City.

For immigrants and visitors to the United States, probably the best-known national monument is the Statue of Liberty on Liberty Island in New York harbor, between the states of New York and New Jersey. The people of France presented the statue to the United States to commemorate the 100th anniversary of the American Revolution. To most people, the statue is a symbol of freedom and escape from oppression.

Statue of Liberty

(Library of Congress)

National parks are usually much larger than national monuments. Their purpose includes the preservation of scenery and wildlife. Some well-known national parks are Yosemite National Park in California; Yellowstone National Park in Idaho, Montana, and Wyoming; and Denali National Park in Alaska.

READING EXERCISE

Read the paragraphs about the geography of the United States. From the information on the map and in the paragraphs, answer the following questions. Check your answers with the answer key on page 185.

1. What does the word *contiguous* mean? _____

_____

2. What ocean is on the west coast of the United States? _____

_____

3. What ocean is on the east coast of the United States?_____

_____

4. The longest and highest mountain range in the United States is the _____.

_____

5. Two states that are on the Canadian border are _____ and _____.

6. Two states on our border with Mexico are _____ and _____.

7. The two longest rivers in the United States are _____ and _____.

8. _____ is the nation's capital.

9. The names of the Great Lakes are _____, _____,

_____, _____, and _____.

10. The largest of the Great Lakes is _____.

11. Two of the five territories of the United States are _____ and

_____.

12. Where is the Statue of Liberty? _____

APPENDIX

FOR READY REFERENCE

Word List

WORD	MEANING
A abbreviation	a shortened form of a word
ability	knowledge and skill needed to do something
abolished	put an end to; did away with
abridge	to make shorter; to lessen
accept	to receive
active	moving; doing one's work, doing things
adjourn	to put off to a later time
administer	to direct or to give
admitted	given the right to enter
adopted	accepted; agreed to; taken as one's own
adult	full-grown; matured
advantage	benefit
advise	inform; tell
afford	to be able to spend money for something
agency	a company or office or organization in business to act for another's benefit
agree	to say "yes"; to have the same opinion
agriculture	the science of farming land
alien	a person from a foreign country; person not yet a citizen
amnesty	a pardon
allegiance	loyalty
allow	to permit
amendment	a change or an addition to a constitution or law
amount	the total sum
annexation	uniting; adding to
anthem	a song or hymn of praise or allegiance
appeal	to take a question from a lower to a higher authority
appeared	was seen; seemed to be
applicant	a person who applies for something
application	a form used to make a request
apply	to ask for something; to let people know you want something
appointed	named to take a job or office
apportion	to make a division
approve	to agree to; to think well of; to say "yes"
area	amount of land; level space

WORD	MEANING
argue	to discuss; to give reasons in support of ideas
arrive	to reach a place; to come
assassinate	to kill or murder suddenly
assemble	to meet together for a common purpose
assistance	help; aid
attorney	a person acting for another person at law
avoid	to keep away from

B

WORD	MEANING
backbone	the most important part
background	the result of training, experience, education
balance	to make equal in value; to make even
base	foundation
basic	serving as a starting point
basis	the main part; supporting element
belief	faith; trust
belongings	things a person owns
benefit	anything that is for the good of a person or thing; money paid to a person
bill	a suggested law proposed by a lawmaker
Bill of Rights	the first ten amendments to the Constitution
borrow	to get something from another person with the understanding that it must be returned
boundary	the line, real or imaginary, that shows where a piece of land ends
brief	short

C

WORD	MEANING
Cabinet	a group of advisers to the president
candidate	a person who runs for office
capital	the city where the government is located
Capitol	the building in which the U.S. Congress meets
cattle	farm animals; livestock
cause	the thing a person fights for; reason
cede	to turn over land usually by treaty
celebrate	to recognize and honor, as a holiday
census	an official count of people
center	a middle point; place where people meet
certificate	a written statement of proof of some fact
character (good)	a good name or a reputation for being responsible and moral
charge	to ask as a price; fee
cheaper	costing less
check	to control; to hold back; to restrain
chief executive	the highest officer of government
choice	a thing preferred; selection
choose	to decide to take; to pick out
circular	a printed paper containing information

WORD	MEANING
citizen	a person having full rights in the place where he or she lives
civil	relating to private rights; having to do with government service
civil service	government work
claim	to ask for as a right
classified ads	short advertisements listed by alphabet in a newspaper
coalition	a partnership or alliance
colonies	settlements in a new land
comfort	something that makes life easier
commerce	trade or business
commissions	small groups of people working for a government
communication	the giving of information
community	a city or town; neighborhood
compare	to show how things are alike or different
compensation	payment for work done or for some other purpose
completes	finishes
comply	to obey
concern	anxiety; interest
condition	how a person or thing is
conduct	to manage; to carry on
Congress	the main law-making body of the United States
conquest	gained by force
consent	to agree; to say "yes"
considers	thinks about; makes allowance for
Constitution	the basic law of the United States
contain	to hold; to have; to include
contiguous	adjoining; next to
continuous	without stopping
contributions	things given to others; gifts
convenience	anything that adds to one's comfort
convention	a meeting for some purpose
conversation	informal talk
costly	expensive; costing a great deal of money
courage	bravery
create	to make
criminal	having to do with a wrongful act against society
crude	rough; not pure

	WORD	MEANING
D	debate	an argument about issues; to take sides in a discussion
	debt	something owed by one person to another or others
	decide	to settle a question
	declaration	a public statement
	Declaration of Independence	a public statement in which the Continental Congress in 1776 said that the 13 colonies were free from Great Britain

WORD	MEANING
Declaration of Intention	a legal paper in which an alien says that he/she intends to become a citizen
declare	to make known openly
defeated	beaten; to win victory over
defense	protection from others
delegate	a person sent to speak or act for others; a representative
democracy	government of, by, and for the people
department	a division or branch of governmental administration
dependent	person needing support—a husband or wife, child, etc.
deposits	material laid down by natural means
deprive	to withhold something from
descendants	children, grandchildren, great-grandchildren
desert	a region without water
destroyed	broken to pieces; ruined; spoiled
difficult	not easy
diploma	a paper that says a person has graduated from a school
disabled	unable to do what most people do; unable to work
disagreement	a difference of opinion; quarrel; dispute
discovered	found
discuss	to talk over
dispute	a heated argument
dissatisfaction	not giving pleasure
dissent	to disagree
district	the part of a state that a congressperson represents
document	written proof
domestic	having to do with our own country; relating to household or family
domestic workers	people who do housework for a living
drug	something taken into the body to help a person get well
due process of law	a limit on the actions of government

E

WORD	MEANING
earn	to make money by working
education	instruction
effect	(used with "in") operational
elected	chosen by the voters
eligible/eligibility	qualified for something; fit to be chosen
emancipate	to free (slaves)
employer	the person or company for whom an individual works
employment	work
energy	power, such as electricity or heat
enforce	to make people do something; to compel
enjoy	to like; to have the benefit of something
equality	sameness in importance; being equal
established	started; set up; founded
examination	a test

WORD	MEANING
examiner	a person who examines or questions another person
exception	a situation that doesn't follow the general rule
exciting	giving great joy; stirring one up
executive	the person who runs things; the boss; executive branch of government that enforces law
exist	to live
expensive	costly
experience	what one has done in the past; anything seen, done, or lived through
export	to send to foreign countries
express	to say; to write; to let people know how one feels or thinks
extended	spread; reached out; made longer

F

factories	places where things are made
fame	being well known
federation	a group in which members are united but keep self-government
fee	a charge for services or privileges; cost
file	to submit an application or a petition
finally	at the end; at last
fingerprint	the mark of a finger that can be used to identify someone
flows	runs like water
formed	organized; developed; came together
former	the one before; the first
founded	started; built for the first time
freedom	not under control by others; to be able to do as one wants
friendly	kindly
function	a duty or job
furnished	having furniture; put in what was needed

G

general	usual; belonging to all
general election	a time when people may vote for any candidate
government	a system of ruling people
graduate	to complete a course of study in a school or college
grant	to give
guarantee	a promise to do something; pledge; stand behind

H

hardships	troubles
headed	led by
hemisphere	half of the world
highway	a main road
hires	employs; gives a job to
honor	to show respect
House of Representatives	the lower house of the U.S. Congress

WORD	MEANING
housing project	a group of houses or apartments in one location

I

WORD	MEANING
immigrant	a newcomer to a country
immunity	freedom from something
impeach	to accuse a public official of misconduct in office
important	meaning much; worthwhile
impress	to make someone remember you; influence
improve	to grow better
include	to form or be a part of something
increase	to become larger
independent	free from control by others
individual	a person
industrial centers	places where there are many factories
ineligible	not qualified
informal	not according to rule; without ceremony; relaxed
information	news; knowledge; facts one learns
informed	to know about; to have knowledge of
institution	organization of a public nature
insures	protects; makes certain; guarantees
intelligence	mental power or ability
intelligent	having knowledge; skilled; able to learn quickly
interesting	holds one's attention
interfere	to enter into the affairs of others; to meddle; to clash
interpret	to help people to understand
interpreter	a person who explains in one language something that was said in a different language
interview	a conversation between an employer and a person who is asking for a job
invaded	entered with the purpose of taking possession
invented	made for the first time
irrigate	to bring water to crops; to water
issue	a problem needing a decision

J

WORD	MEANING
judicial	having to do with courts and judges and interpreting the laws
jurisdiction	control
jury	a group of people sworn to hear the evidence and give a decision in a case

K

WORD	MEANING
knowledge	information; news; facts

L

WORD	MEANING
landlord	a person who owns an apartment house or other rental property
lawfully	according to the law
lease	an agreement to rent a house or apartment

WORD	MEANING
legal	correct according to law; having to do with law
legislation	making and passing laws
legislative	having to do with making laws
legislature	the lawmaking body
lending	allowing the use of something for a while
level	even
librarian	the person in charge of a library
library	a building containing a collection of books; also a collection of books
license	to authorize by legal permit
listed	written in order
living	being alive
local	nearby; in one's own neighborhood or city
located	in; in a certain place
loyal	true to one's friends or country

M

majority	most; more than half of those voting
manufacture	to make, usually in a factory
marital	having to do with being married
member	a person who is part of a group of people
mine	a pit from which coal or ore is dug
minimum	the smallest number or amount
miracle	a remarkable thing or event
mode	the way in which something is done
moral	having to do with right and wrong
motor vehicle	a car, automobile, or truck
mourned	felt sad

N

narrow	limited; not wide
native-born	born in the country where a person lives
naturalization hearing	an examination of an applicant for citizenship
naturalized	admitted to citizenship
necessary	needed; essential
needy	poor; not having enough to live on
neighbor	a person living near another person
neighborhood	a place where people live near one another; community
newcomer	a person in this country for a short time; an alien
nominate	to name or propose for office
nominee	a person named as a candidate for office
notice	to see; a written or printed sign giving information or warning; announcement

O

oath	a solemn promise of the truth of a statement
occupation	the kind of work a person does
official	an officer holding a government job; formal

WORD	MEANING
operate	to work; to act
opinion	a particular judgment or belief; what one thinks
opportunity	a chance to do or get something
ore	rock, sand, or dirt having some metal in it
organize	to get people together for a purpose; to plan

P pamphlet .... a little booklet

participate	to take part or share in
pension	regular payment of living expenses to a person who has retired
permanent	steady; lasting; fixed
permit	to allow
persecute	to treat someone cruelly because of his or her beliefs
persecution	cruel treatment of a person because of his or her beliefs
petition	a formal written request
physical	having to do with the body
Pilgrims	settlers who came from England and founded the colony of Plymouth in 1620
plantation	a farm or estate
Pledge of Allegiance	a formal statement of loyalty to the government
political opinion	a general thought on what is going on in government
politician	a person who works for a political party
politics	affairs of government; management of political affairs
polls	places where people vote
population	people; the number of people in a place
posterity	future generations
postmaster	the person in charge of a post office
poultry	chickens, turkeys, geese, ducks
power	a strong nation; strength; might; force
preamble	the opening part of a statement
precious	dear; of great value
prefer	to like one thing better than another; to choose; to decide in favor of
prescription	a written order to a druggist telling him or her to make a certain medicine according to a physician's directions
preserve	to keep
prey	to attack; a victim, or one who is helpless under attack
primary election	a time when people nominate, rather than elect, a candidate
principal	main; most important; chief
private	belonging to or concerning an individual; personal; one's own; not public
privately owned	owned by individuals, rather than a community
privilege	a benefit or advantage
problems	questions
process	a series of actions

WORD	MEANING
proclamation	an official public announcement or notice; official publication
produce	to make or manufacture; to grow
products	things made or grown for use
professional	describing a job requiring special education
prohibits	does not permit; forbids
proper	right; correct
protection	providing safety; keeping a person or thing from being harmed
proud	thinking well of oneself
provides	gives; makes possible
public	belonging to the people of a community, state, or nation; not private
public housing projects	a group of houses built by the city, state, or federal government
public office	a position in the service of a nation, state, or city
purposes	reasons for doing something

Q qualification .... a requirement

R

ratify	to approve
reasons	explanations
receipt	a written statement that someone has received something
record	a thing written or kept for future use
references	letters from employers saying how good a worker a person is
refineries	places where raw materials are made ready for use
refugee	a person who leaves a country because of persecution
regarding	about
region	an area; section of a country or state
register	to have one's name written into a list of people who can take a job or can vote
regularly	at certain, expected times
relatives	people in one's own family
religious	relating to faith and worship
remind	to tell again
rent	to pay for the use of land, home, property; the money paid for such use
represent	to speak and work for a person or a group of people
representative	a person chosen to act for another; delegate
republic	a system of representative government
requirement	something needed
residence	a place where a person lives
resource	any supply that will meet a need
respect	to show honor
responsibility	a task; a debt; a duty

WORD	MEANING
retire	to give up a job or office; to stop working
right	something to which one has a just claim; any power or privilege given a person by law, custom, etc.
rivals	individuals who are opponents
rule	to guide; to govern; to control

S

WORD	MEANING
sanitation	keeping things clean for health reasons
secret	known only to oneself
security	safety; financial comfort
seeking	looking for
segregate	to separate (often by force) one group of people from others
select	to choose
self-educated	taught by oneself
Senate	the upper house of the U.S. Congress
separate	to keep apart; describing things kept apart
separation of powers	duties that have no connection with each other
service	a convenience; a useful thing to be done or given; a helpful act
service trades	jobs that make other people more comfortable
settle	to set up a home; to live
share	to use and enjoy together
shortage	too small a number or amount; not enough
shorthand	writing by symbols
skill	great ability
slavery	the owning or keeping of slaves
slogan	a group of words making the purpose of something clear
Social Security	a federal plan to take care of workers in their old age
solved	figured out; found the answer
source	a place where something comes from
specialized	different; unusual; requiring special training
spouse	wife or husband
standard of living	a way of living; things needed and used in order to live in a certain way
"Star-Spangled Banner"	the national anthem of the United States
stationery	articles such as paper, pens, ink, pencils, etc.
stenography	writing in shorthand
strange	not known or heard of before
strength	ability; force; power
structure	a framework, a building
struggle	to battle; fight
suffrage	the right to vote
suggests	hints; mentions
supply	to give, provide, or fill
supreme	highest in importance
surveyor	a person who measures and marks land

WORD	MEANING
survived	lived after others died
sworn	bound by oath
symbol	an object that stands for something else
system of checks and balances	a system in which each branch of government has powers that to some degree control the powers of others

T

WORD	MEANING
technological	relating to science and industry
tenant	a person who rents an apartment, house, etc. from another person or from a landlord
territory	land; region; land belonging to a government
textiles	woven cloth
trade	business; work one does
trained	taught; made ready and able to do something
traitor	a person who works against his own country
tranquility	the condition of being calm, peaceful, or quiet
treasury	the country's money
treaty	agreement between nations
tuition	money paid to a school in order to attend it
type	kind; sort; to typewrite

U

WORD	MEANING
unalienable	cannot be taken away or lessened
unconstitutional	not according to the Constitution or law
undocumented	without legal documents
uneducated	not trained; unskilled
union	people joined together for a common purpose
unity	being together; being or acting as one
unusual	not common; rare
uphold	to support
urban	relating to a city or town

V

WORD	MEANING
vacancy	an empty apartment, house, or room that can be rented; a job that is open
valid	having force in law
veto	to refuse to allow a bill to become a law by not signing it
vocational	having to do with trades
void	not in force

W

WORD	MEANING
want	to need; something needed
wealth	riches; land; resources; money
welcome	a greeting
wise	to have great understanding of persons, conditions, and situations
witnesses	those who give testimony and evidence
wonder	to think about; want to know why
worship	to pray to; to pay honor and respect to

American English: Idiomatic Expressions

The American language and customs often are difficult for students. Many teachers find that their pupils encounter unnecessary difficulty with the examination for naturalization. This section provides specific American English language practice and orientation.

The non-English speaker in the United States, or the newcomer of limited educational background, has difficulty facing differences in language and culture, especially within the context of the naturalization examinations. Everybody has the same problem. Even if you have overcome the basic differences and are on your way to fluency in the new language, you will be helped by the step-by-step presentation in this guide.

For the most part, the naturalization examination is an oral test. The examiner asks the questions; you answer them. Your answer depends on how you interpret the question. If the examiner uses expressions you don't understand, you may be *at a loss!* You can see how important it is to become familiar with different patterns of American speech and with a wide range of special expressions that Americans use as part of their everyday lives. When you practice using these expressions yourself, you will become more confident and successful in your own everyday exchanges with natural-born Americans. Success breeds success! Does that *ring a bell* with you? Of course! *It figures* that this new fluency will help you reach one more step *up the ladder* of success to community participation and, eventually, to real citizenship.

Idioms are groups of words used together in a special sense. They are expressions regularly used in that certain way. There are four examples in what you have just read. The meanings are easy. Say them now—say the entire sentence out loud. Then repeat only the idioms. That's it!

Another example that may help before you study the lists comes from my own experience as a teacher of English.

One day, one of my students raised his hand to ask, "What is a teasy?"

"Do you mean a tease?" I asked.

"Not a tease! A teasy, I hear it all the time. In the subway, many people push and shove. Then some people say, "Take a Teasy!"

I explained the meaning of *take it easy.* And my student was happy.

Take it easy is a common American expression.

Of course, you know that it means to relax, slow down. Another idiom like it is *easy does it.* Say them both now. Make them part of your language!

More Common Idioms

Word	Idiom	Meaning
according	according to	— on the authority
all	all right	— satisfactory
	all at once, all of a sudden	— unexpectedly
	all day (night, week, month)	— continuously
along	go along with	— agree (with an idea)
	get along with	— agree (with a person)
as	as a matter of fact	— really
	as soon as	— when
at	at all (not at all)	— to any degree
be	be over	— finished
bear	bear in mind (keep in mind)	— remember
break	break down	— fall apart
	breakdown	— failure to function
by	by heart	— by memory
	by myself	— alone
	by the way	— incidentally
call	call on	— request help from, visit
	call up	— telephone
catch	catch cold	— get a cold
	catch fire	— get on fire, burn
change	change of $10	— money
	change one's mind	— decide differently
charge	in charge of	— be responsible for
	be charged with (robbery, murder, etc.)	— having a statement made against
count	count on	— depend
cover	to cover up	— to hide something
	cover-up	— something concealed
cross	to cross the street	— to go across
	to cross out	— to draw a line through
day	day off	— nonworking day
	day in, day out	— all the time
do	to do one's best	— to try hard
	what do you *do?*	— what is your work? (answer: *I'm a* lawyer, plumber, etc.)
	do over	— to correct

Word	**Idiom**	**Meaning**
else	what else, where else	— besides the answer given
entitled	to be entitled to	— to deserve (by law)
every	every now and then	— from time to time
	every other day	— on two days with a day in between
figure out	can you figure out the meaning?	— estimate, determine
file	to file a claim, a report, document	— to turn over a paper to the proper authority
fill	fill in (the form, etc.), fill out	— to put in what is necessary
find	to find out	— to learn
for	for the present, for the time being	— temporarily
fringe	fringe benefits .	— special good things that go with some jobs
get	to get along	— to succeed
	to get along with	— to be friends with
	to get away with	— to escape
	to get in touch with	— to communicate with
going	going to (in the future)	— will go, will do something
had	had better	— it would be a good idea to
hand	hand in	— to submit a paper
	on hand	— in stock
hang	to hang up	— to put back
hear	to hear from	— to get word from
hold	to hold on	— to wait
	to hold off	— to delay
in	in a hurry	— in a rush
	in the long run	— over a long period of time
	in time	— soon enough
just	just a minute	— soon
	just so	— correct
keep	to keep an eye on	— to watch
	to keep in touch with	— to continue communication
	to keep up	— to continue
know	to know by heart	— to memorize
lay	to lay off	— to get let go from a job
little	little by little	— gradually

Word	Idiom	Meaning
look	to look after	— to care for
	to look forward to	— to anticipate
	to look into	— to check
	to look up	— to search for
make	to make an appointment	— to set a date for
	to make clear	— to explain
meet	to meet the requirements	— to be eligible
mixed	mixed up	— confused
more	more or less	— for the most part
never	never mind	— forget it
nothing	nothing wrong,	— everything is okay
	nothing the matter	
now	now and then	— once in a while
on	on the radio, television, etc.	— in a program
	on time	— punctual
out	out of order	— not functioning
	out of the question	— not possible
over	do it over and over	— to repeat something many times
pass	pass judgment on	— give an opinion on
	pass a law	— enact a bill
	to pass away	— to die
pick	pick out	— choose
	to pick up	— to take
play	to play ball	— to go along with
point	to point out	— to call attention to
put	to put down	— to suppress
	to put on	— to assume
	to put off	— to postpone
quiet	quiet down	— stop making noise or speaking
quite	quite a few	— many
rather	rather than	— instead of
responsible	responsible for	— in charge of
right	right away	— very soon
say	say the word	— give the order
	to say nothing of	— not to mention
scam	to pull a scam	— trick to deceive

Word	Idiom	Meaning
see	to see about	— to check into
	to see to it	— to ensure
take	take an oath	— swear
	take one's time	— go slowly
think	think it over	— consider it carefully
time	to have time	— plenty of time left
up	up-to-date	— timely
used	used to	— in the past
vain	in vain	— without success
very	the very thing	— exactly right
walk	to walk out	— to leave
while	a little while	— a short time
without	to do without	— to lack
work	to work out	— to exercise
write	to write away for	— to send for

As you can see, English is an idiomatic language. These are only a sample of those you may hear in everyday speech.

REVIEW

As a review, see if you can fill in the blanks in the following sentences with an idiomatic expression from the list.

1. I_____live in Chicago, but now I live in New York.

2. I_____to pay my taxes; they are not due until April.

3. It is_____for me to lend my friend money at this time.

4. Business is so bad, the company will have to _____ some

   workers.

5. Joe worked in a dress factory for_____last year.

6. Please_____for an application for me!

7. Olga is_____to bringing her husband into this

   country soon.

8. She_____him last week that his application was being

   checked.

9. "_____, it takes time," said Olga's teacher.

10. "He will have a nervous_____ if he doesn't get his papers

soon," she answered.

Check your answer to these questions with the answer key on page 185.

American English: Pronunciation Practice

Even after many years in their new country, some immigrants still experience difficulties with the *consonant sounds* of American English. If you have problems with Ls, Rs, Bs, Hs, Vs, Th blends, and others, this section is for you.

Practice, practice the positions of the mouth, lips, and tongue, in order to produce the sound correctly. Exaggerate the directions. Use a mirror. In any case, do it every day!

	Say	*Repeat*
Beginning L and R Sounds		
Put tip of tongue	let	Let Lulu do it.
behind upper teeth.	light	Light the lamp.
	right	The answer is right.
	run	Run the race.
T and D, N and S		
Put tip of tongue above	tell	Tell me the time.
upper front teeth.	tight	Too tight.
	don't	Don't run!
	did	Did Dot do her lesson?
	dull	It was too dull.
	no, not	Not at all!
	sunset	The sun sets late in Sweden.
TH		
Open lips a little; put	the	This is the time
tongue between teeth.	this	to think about supper.
	think	

CH, SH, Y, J, and Z
Put middle of tongue
against top of mouth.

chin	Place your chin on the ship
ship	in the bottle.
join	Charles and John joined the
	union yesterday.
measure	Measure the chair to see if it is
	larger than the old chair.

H Sound
Part your lips and blow.

he	He asked her to show him
her	her new home.
home	

M, P, B, and W (WH) Sounds
Bring your lips together.

Mama	The baby's first word
move	was *Papa,* not *Mama.*
Papa	What will you do?
baby	Where will you go?
will	
what, where	

F and V
Bite your lower lip.

fat	The very fat man wants
very	to be thin.

K, X, G, and NG
Put back of tongue against
top of mouth.

key	Keep the exit door locked
exit	with a key.
girl	The girl keeps singing a
sing a song	song all day long.

This is a simple approach to some sounds that may be difficult for you. Practice them as often as you can. You will be glad when it is time for your naturalization examination!

National Holidays

You may be asked why we celebrate the national holiday nearest to the time of your naturalization examination. You may wonder why businesses have special sales on February 22. Of course, you know that the Fourth of July/Independence Day is our most important national holiday. Do you know why the following holidays are celebrated nationally?

January 1	New Year's Day
January 15*	Birthday of Martin Luther King, Jr.
February 22*	Presidents' Day (Birthday of George Washington)
May 30*	Memorial Day
July 4	The Fourth of July/Independence Day
First Monday in September	Labor Day
October 12*	Columbus Day
November 11	Veterans Day
Fourth Thursday in November	Thanksgiving Day
December 25	Christmas

*These holidays are celebrated on the closest Monday to give people a three-day weekend. And, if the holiday falls on a Sunday, the next day also is celebrated as a holiday.

Special Observances

These are not holidays, but special observances are held in different parts of the United States on these days.

February 12	Lincoln's Birthday
February 14	St. Valentine's Day
March 17	St. Patrick's Day
Second Sunday in May	Mother's Day
June 14	Flag Day
Third Sunday in June	Father's Day
September 17	Citizenship Day
October 24	United Nations Day
First Tuesday after first Monday in November	Election Day

Religious holy dates, of course, also are widely observed.

REVIEW: Holidays and Observances

Read the dates in Column I aloud. Then read Column II. Match the letters with the numbers by drawing lines from one to the other. Lastly, put the letters in the space next to the numbered items. Do it like this:

1. Fourth Thursday   <u>c</u>   **c.** Thanksgiving Day
in November

COLUMN I		COLUMN II
1. October 12	___	**a.** St. Patrick's Day
2. December 25	___	**b.** Labor Day
3. March 17	___	**c.** Martin Luther King Jr.'s Birthday
4. January 15	___	**d.** Veterans Day
5. First Monday in September	___	**e.** Columbus Day
6. February 22	___	**f.** Lincoln's Birthday
7. June 14	___	**g.** Memorial Day
8. July 4	___	**h.** Flag Day
9. February 12	___	**i.** George Washington's Birthday
10. May 30	___	**j.** Christmas Day
	___	**k.** Independence Day

Turn the book upside down to find the right answers.

ANSWERS
1. e.
2. j.
3. a.
4. c.
5. b.
6. i.
7. h.
8. k.
9. f.
10. g.

The Declaration of Independence

In Congress, July 4, 1776

THE UNANIMOUS DECLARATION OF THE THIRTEEN UNITED STATES OF AMERICA

When, in the Course of human events, it becomes necessary for one people to dissolve the political bands which have connected them with another, and to assume among the powers of the earth, the separate and equal station to which the Laws of Nature and of Nature's God entitle them, a decent respect to the opinions of mankind requires that they should declare the causes which impel them to the separation.

We hold these truths to be self-evident, that all men are created equal, that they are endowed by their Creator with certain unalienable Rights, that among these, are Life, Liberty, and the pursuit of Happiness. That, to secure these rights, Governments are instituted among Men, deriving their just powers from the consent of the governed, that, whenever any Form of Government becomes destructive of these ends, it is the Right of the People to alter or to abolish it, and to institute new Government, laying its foundation on such principles, and organizing its powers in such form, as to them shall seem likely to effect their Safety and Happiness. Prudence, indeed, will dictate that Governments long established, should not be changed for light and transient causes; and, accordingly, all experience hath shown, that mankind are more disposed to suffer, while evils are sufferable, than to right themselves by abolishing the forms to which they are accustomed. But, when a long train of abuses and usurpations, pursuing invariably the same Object, evinces a design to reduce them under absolute Despotism, it is their right, it is their duty, to throw off such Government and to provide new Guards for their future security.—Such has been the patient sufferance of these Colonies; and such is now the necessity which constrains them to alter their former Systems of Government. The history of the present King of Great Britain is a history of repeated injuries and usurpations, all having in direct object the establishment of an absolute Tyranny over these States. To prove this, let Facts be submitted to a candid world.—

He has refused his Assent to Laws the most wholesome and necessary for the public good.

He has forbidden his Governors to pass Laws of immediate and pressing importance, unless suspended in their operation till his Assent should be obtained; and when so suspended, he has utterly neglected to attend to them.

He has refused to pass other laws for the accommodation of large districts of people, unless those people would relinquish the right of Representation in the Legislature; a right inestimable to them and formidable to tyrants only.

He has called together legislative bodies at places unusual, uncomfortable, and distant from the depository of their public Records, for the sole purpose of fatiguing them into compliance with his measures.

He has dissolved Representative Houses repeatedly, for opposing with manly firmness his invasions on the rights of the people.

He has refused for a long time, after such dissolutions, to cause others to be elected; whereby the Legislative powers, incapable of Annihilation, have returned to the People at large for their exercise; the State remaining, in the meantime, exposed to all the dangers of invasion from without, and convulsions within.

He has endeavored to prevent the population of these States; for that purpose, obstructing the Laws for Naturalization of Foreigners; refusing to pass others to encourage their migrations hither, and raising the conditions of new Appropriations of Lands.

He has obstructed the Administration of Justice, by refusing his Assent to Laws for establishing Judiciary powers.

He has made Judges dependent on his Will alone, for the tenure of their offices, and the amount and payment of their salaries.

He has erected a multitude of New Offices, and sent hither swarms of Officers to harass our people, and eat out their substance.

He has kept among us, in times of peace, Standing Armies, without the Consent of our legislatures.

He has affected to render the Military independent of, and superior to, the Civil power.

He has combined, with others, to subject us to a jurisdiction foreign to our constitution, and unacknowledged by our laws; giving his Assent to their Acts of pretended Legislation:

For quartering large bodies of armed troops among us:

For protecting them by a mock Trial, from punishment, for any Murders which they should commit on the Inhabitants of these States:

For cutting off our Trade with all parts of the world:

For imposing Taxes on us without our Consent:

For depriving us, in many cases, of the benefits of Trial by Jury:

For transporting us beyond Seas to be tried for pretended offenses:

For abolishing the free System of English Laws in a neighboring Province, establishing therein an Arbitrary government, and enlarging its Boundaries, so as to render it at once an example and fit instrument for introducing the same absolute rule into these Colonies:

For taking away our Charters, abolishing our most valuable Laws, and altering, fundamentally, the Forms of our Governments:

For suspending our own Legislatures, and declaring themselves invested with power to legislate for us in all cases whatsoever.

He has abdicated Government here, by declaring us out of his Protection, and waging War against us.

He has plundered our seas, ravaged our Coasts, burnt our towns, and destroyed the lives our our people.

He is, at this time, transporting large Armies of foreign Mercenaries to complete the works of death, desolation, and tyranny, already begun with circumstances of Cruelty & perfidy scarcely paralleled in the most barbarous ages, and totally unworthy the Head of a civilized nation.

He has constrained our fellow Citizens, taken Captive on the high Seas, to bear Arms against their Country, to become the executioners of their friends and Brethren, or to fall themselves by their Hands.

He has excited domestic insurrections amongst us, and has endeavored to bring on the inhabitants of our frontiers, the merciless Indian Savages, whose known rule of warfare, is, an undistinguished destruction of all ages, sexes and conditions.

In every stage of these Oppressions, We have Petitioned for Redress, in the most humble terms; our repeated Petitions have been answered only by repeated injury. A Prince, whose character is thus marked by every act which may define a Tyrant, is unfit to be the ruler of a free people.

Nor have we been wanting in attentions to our British brethren. We have warned them, from time to time, of attempts made by their legislature to extend an unwarrantable jurisdiction over us. We have reminded them of the circumstances of our emigration and settlement here. We have appealed to their native justice and magnanimity, and we have conjured them by the ties of our common kindred to disavow these usurpations, which would inevitably interrupt our connections and correspondence. They too have been deaf to the voice of justice and of consanguinity. We must, therefore, acquiesce in the necessity, which denounces our Separation, and hold them, as we hold the rest of mankind, Enemies in War, in Peace Friends.

We, therefore, the Representatives of the united States of America, in General Congress, Assembled, appealing to the Supreme Judge of the world for the rectitude of our intentions, do, in the Name, and by Authority of the good People of these Colonies, solemnly publish and declare, That these United Colonies are, and of Right ought to be, Free and Independent States; that they are Absolved from all Allegiance to the British Crown, and that all political connection between them and the State of Great Britain is, and ought to be, totally dissolved: and that, as Free and Independent States, they have full Power to levy War, conclude Peace, contract Alliances, establish Commerce, and to do all other Acts and Things which Independent States may of right do. And, for the support of this Declaration, with a firm reliance on the protection of divine Providence, we mutually pledge to each other our Lives, our Fortunes, and our sacred Honor.

The foregoing Declaration was, by order of Congress, engrossed, and signed by the following members:

John Hancock
(Massachusetts Bay)

New Hampshire
Josiah Bartlett, William Whipple, Matthew Thornton

Massachusetts Bay
Samuel Adams, John Adams, Robert Treat Paine, Elbridge Gerry

Rhode Island
Stephen Hopkins, William Ellery

Connecticut
Roger Sherman, Samuel Huntington, William Williams, Oliver Wolcott

New York
William Floyd, Philip Livingston, Francis Lewis, Lewis Morris

New Jersey
Richard Stockton, John Witherspoon, Francis Hopkinson, John Hart, Abraham Clark

Pennsylvania
Robert Morris, Benjamin Rush, Benjamin Franklin, John Morton, George Clymer, James Smith, George Taylor, James Wilson, George Ross

Delaware
Caesar Rodney, George Read, Thomas McKean

Maryland
Samuel Chase, William Paca, Thomas Stone, Charles Carroll of Carrollton

Virginia
George Wythe, Richard Henry Lee, Thomas Jefferson, Benjamin Harrison, Thomas Nelson, Jr., Francis Lightfoot Lee, Carter Braxton

North Carolina
William Hooper, Joseph Hewes, John Penn

South Carolina
Edward Rutledge, Thomas Heyward, Jr., Thomas Lynch, Jr., Arthur Middleton

Georgia
Button Gwinnett, Lyman Hall, George Walton

RESOLVED, That copies of the Declaration be sent to the several assemblies, conventions, and committees, or councils of safety, and to the several commanding officers of the continental troops; that it be proclaimed in each of the united States, at the head of the army.

The Constitution of the United States

PREAMBLE

WE THE PEOPLE of the United States, in Order to form a more perfect Union, establish Justice, insure domestic Tranquility, provide for the common defense, promote the general Welfare, and secure the Blessings of Liberty to ourselves and our Posterity, do ordain and establish this CONSTITUTION for the United States of America.

General objectives of the Constitution

ARTICLE I • LEGISLATIVE DEPARTMENT

SECTION 1. All legislative Powers herein granted shall be vested in a Congress of the United States, which shall consist of a Senate and House of Representatives.

A bicameral Congress

SECTION 2. [1]The House of Representatives shall be composed of Members chosen every second Year by the People of the several States, and the Electors in each State shall have the Qualifications requisite for Electors of the most numerous Branch of the State Legislature.

Selection and term of Representatives

[2]No person shall be a representative who shall not have attained to the Age of twenty five Years, and been seven Years a Citizen of the United States, and who shall not, when elected, be an Inhabitant of that State in which he shall be chosen.

Qualifications of Representatives

[3][Representatives and direct Taxes shall be apportioned among the several States which may be included within this Union, according to their respective Numbers, which shall be determined by adding to the whole Number of free Persons, including those bound to Service for a Term of Years, and excluding Indians not taxed, three fifths of all other Persons.].* The actual Enumeration shall be made within three Years after the first Meeting of the Congress of the United States, and within every subsequent Term of ten Years, in such Manner as they shall by Law direct. The Number of Representatives shall not exceed one for every thirty Thousand, but each State shall have at Least one Representative; and until such enumeration shall be made, the State of New Hampshire shall be entitled to choose three, Massachusetts eight, Rhode-Island and Providence Plantations one, Connecticut five, New York six, New Jersey four, Pennsylvania eight, Delaware one, Maryland six, Virginia ten, North Carolina five, South Carolina five, and Georgia three.

Apportionment of Representatives among states—see Section 2 of Fourteenth Amendment: a decennial census; maximum and minimum size of House

[4]When vacancies happen in the Representation from any State, the Executive Authority thereof shall issue Writs of Election to fill such Vacancies.

Filling of vacancies

[5]The House of Representatives shall choose their Speaker and other Officers; and shall have the sole Power of Impeachment.

Choice of Speaker and other officers; sole power of impeachment

---

Note:—This text of the Constitution follows the engrossed copy signed by Gen. Washington and the deputies from 12 States. The superior number preceding the paragraphs designates the number of the clause; it was not in the original. Also, some spellings have been changed from the original for ease of reading.
* The part included in square brackets was changed by Section 2 of the Fourteenth Amendment. Spellings have been modernized.

Composition of Senate; see Seventeenth Amendment for selection of Senators. Terms of Senators— overlapping

SECTION 3.   [1]The Senate of the United States shall be composed of two Senators from each State, [chosen by the Legislature thereof,]* for six Years; and each senator shall have one Vote.

[2]Immediately after they shall be assembled in Consequence of the first Election, they shall be divided as equally as may be into three Classes. The Seats of the Senators of the first Class shall be vacated at the Expiration of the second Year, of the second Class at the Expiration of the fourth Year, and of the third Class at the Expiration of the sixth Year, so that one third may be chosen every second Year; [and if Vacancies happen by Resignation, or otherwise, during the Recess of the Legislature of any State, the Executive thereof may make temporary Appointments until the next Meeting of the Legislature, which shall then fill such Vacancies].**

Vacancies—see Seventeenth Amendment

Qualifications

[3]No Person shall be a Senator who shall not have attained to the Age of thirty Years, and been nine Years a Citizen of the United States, and who shall not, when elected, be an Inhabitant of that State for which he shall be chosen.

Vice President to preside; choice of other officers

[4]The Vice President of the United States shall be President of the Senate, but shall have no Vote, unless they be equally divided.

[5]The Senate shall choose their other Officers, and also a President pro tempore, in the Absence of the Vice President, or when he shall exercise the Office of President of the United States.

Trial of impeachment by Senate; penalties if impeached and convicted.

[6]The Senate shall have the sole Power to try all Impeachments. When sitting for that Purpose, they shall be on Oath or Affirmation. When the President of the United States is tried, the Chief Justice shall preside: And no Person shall be convicted without the Concurrence of two thirds of the Members present.

[7]Judgment in Cases of Impeachment shall not extend further than to removal from Office, and disqualification to hold and enjoy any Office of honor, Trust or Profit under the United States: but the Party convicted shall nevertheless be liable and subject to Indictment, Trial, Judgment and Punishment, according to Law.

Times, places, and manner of holding Congressional elections.

SECTION 4.   [1]The Times, Places and Manner of holding Elections for Senators and Representatives, shall be prescribed in each State by the Legislature thereof; but the Congress may at any time by Law make or alter such Regulations, except as to the Places of choosing Senators.

Congressional sessions— see Twentieth Amendment

[2]The Congress shall assemble at Least once in every Year, and such Meeting shall [be on the first Monday in December,]*** unless they shall by Law appoint a different Day.

Judging elections and qualifications; size of a quorum; expulsion of members of Congress

SECTION 5.   [1]Each House shall be the Judge of the Elections, Returns and Qualifications of its own Members, and a Majority of each shall constitute a Quorum to do Business; but a smaller Number may adjourn from day to day, and

---

*The part included in square brackets was changed by Clause 2 of the Seventeenth Amendment.
**The part included in square brackets was changed by Section 2 of the Seventeenth Amendment.
***The part included in square brackets was changed by Section 2 of the Twentieth Amendment.

may be authorized to compel the Attendance of absent Members, in such Manner, and under such Penalties as each House may provide.

[2]Each House may determine the Rules of its Proceedings, punish its Members for disorderly Behavior, and, with the Concurrence of two thirds, expel a Member.

Rules of proceeding and keeping of journal.

[3]Each House shall keep a Journal of its Proceedings, and from time to time publish the same, excepting such Parts as may in their Judgment require Secrecy; and the Yeas and Nays of the Members of either House on any question shall, at the Desire of one fifth of those Present, be entered on the Journal.

[4]Neither House, during the Session of Congress, shall, without the Consent of the other, adjourn for more than three days, nor to any other Place than that in which the two Houses shall be sitting.

Adjournment

SECTION 6.   [1]The Senators and Representatives shall receive a Compensation for their Services, to be ascertained by Law, and paid out of the Treasury of the United States. They shall in all Cases, except Treason, Felony and Breach of the Peace, be privileged from Arrest during their Attendance at the Session of their respective Houses, and in going to and returning from the same; and for any Speech or Debate in either House, they shall not be questioned in any other Place.

Compensation and immunities of members of Congress

[2]No Senator or Representative shall, during the Time for which he was elected, be appointed to any civil Office under the Authority of the United States, which shall have been created, or the Emoluments whereof shall have been increased during such time; and no Person holding any Office under the United States, shall be a Member of either House during his Continuance in Office.

Limitations on appointment of members of Congress to civil offices; no national office-holder to be a member of Congress

SECTION 7.   [1]All Bills for raising Revenue shall originate in the House of Representatives; but the Senate may propose or concur with Amendments as on other Bills.

Origin of revenue bills

[2]Every Bill which shall have passed the House of Representatives and the Senate, shall, before it becomes a Law, be presented to the President of the United States; If he approve he shall sign it, but if not he shall return it, with his Objections to that House in which it shall have originated, who shall enter the Objections at large on their Journal, and proceed to reconsider it. If after such Reconsideration two thirds of that House shall agree to pass the Bill, it shall be sent, together with the Objections, to the other House, by which it shall likewise be reconsidered, and if approved by two thirds of that House, it shall become a Law. But in all such Cases the Votes of both Houses shall be determined by Yeas and Nays, and the Names of the Persons voting for and against the Bill shall be entered on the Journal of each House respectively. If any Bill shall not be returned by the President within ten days (Sundays excepted) after it shall have been presented to him, the Same shall be a Law, in like Manner as if he had signed it, unless the Congress by their Adjournment prevent its Return, in which Case it shall not be a Law.

Veto power of President: overriding of veto

[3]Every Order, Resolution, or Vote to which the Concurrence of the Senate and House of Representatives may be necessary (except on a question of Adjournment) shall be presented to the President of the United States; and before the Same shall take Effect, shall be approved by him, or being disapproved by him,

shall be repassed by two thirds of the Senate and House of Representatives, according to the Rules and Limitations prescribed in the Case of a Bill.

Enumerated powers of Congress: Taxation

SECTION 8.   [1]The Congress shall have Power To lay and collect Taxes, Duties, Imposts and Excises, to pay the Debts and provide for the common Defense and general Welfare of the United States; but all Duties, Imposts and Excises shall be uniform throughout the United States;

Borrowing of money

[2]To borrow Money on the credit of the United States;

Regulation of commerce

[3]To regulate Commerce with foreign Nations, and among the several States, and with the Indian Tribes;

Naturalization and bankruptcy

[4]To establish a uniform Rule of Naturalization, and uniform Laws on the subject of Bankruptcies throughout the United States;

Coining of money; weights and measures

[5]To coin Money, regulate the Value thereof, and of foreign Coin, and fix the Standard of Weights and Measures;

Punishment of counterfeiting

[6]To provide for the Punishment of counterfeiting the Securities and current Coin of the United States;

Postal service

[7]To establish Post Offices and post Roads;

Patents and copyrights

[8]To promote the Progress of Science and useful Arts, by securing for limited Times to Authors and Inventors the exclusive Right to their respective Writings and Discoveries;

Creation of courts

[9]To constitute Tribunals inferior to the supreme Court;

Piracies and high seas felonies

[10]To define and punish Piracies and Felonies committed on the high Seas, and Offenses against the Law of Nations;

[11]To declare War, grant Letters of Marque and Reprisal, and make Rules concerning Captures on Land and Water;

Declaration of War

[12]To raise and support Armies, but no Appropriation of Money to that Use shall be for a longer Term than two Years;

Provide armed forces and for calling forth and organizing the militia

[13]To provide and maintain a Navy;

[14]To make Rules for the Government and Regulation of the land and naval Forces;

[15]To provide for calling forth the Militia to execute the Laws of the Union, suppress Insurrections and repel Invasions;

[16]To provide for organizing, arming, and disciplining the Militia and for governing such Part of them as may be employed in the Service of the United States, reserving to the States respectively, the Appointment of the Officers, and the Authority of training the Militia according to the discipline prescribed by Congress;

Congress to govern the District of Columbia and other places owned by national government

[17]To exercise exclusive Legislation in all Cases whatsoever, over such District (not exceeding ten Miles square) as may, by Cession of particular States, and the Acceptance of Congress, become the Seat of the Government of the United States, and to exercise like Authority over all Places purchased by the Consent of the Legislature of the State in which the Same shall be, for the Erection of Forts, Magazines, Arsenals, dock-Yards, and other needful Buildings;—And

[18]To make all Laws which shall be necessary and proper for carrying into Execution the foregoing Powers, and all other Powers vested by this Constitution in the Government of the United States, or in any Department or Officer thereof.

Necessary and proper (elastic) clause

SECTION 9.   [1]The Migration or Importation of such Persons as any of the States now existing shall think proper to admit, shall not be prohibited by the Congress prior to the Year one thousand eight hundred and eight, but a Tax or duty may be imposed on such Importation, not exceeding ten dollars for each Person.

Express limitations on national government— Congress in particular

[2]The Privilege of the Writ of Habeas Corpus shall not be suspended, unless when in Cases of Rebellion or Invasion the public Safety may require it.

[3]No Bill of Attainder or ex post facto Law shall be passed.

*[4]No Capitation, or other direct, Tax shall be laid, unless in Proportion to the Census or Enumeration herein before directed to be taken.

[5]No Tax or Duty shall be laid on Articles exported from any State.

[6]No Preference shall be given by any Regulation of Commerce or Revenue to the Ports of one State over those of another: nor shall Vessels bound to, or from, one State be obliged to enter, clear, or pay Duties in another.

[7]No Money shall be drawn from the Treasury, but in Consequence of Appropriations made by Law; and a regular Statement and Account of the Receipts and Expenditures of all public Money shall be published from time to time.

[8]No Title of Nobility shall be granted by the United States: And no Person holding any Office of Profit or Trust under them, shall, without the Consent of the Congress, accept of any present, Emolument, Office, or Title, of any kind of whatever, from any King, Prince, or foreign State.

SECTION 10.   [1]No State shall enter into any Treaty, Alliance, or Confederation; grant Letters of Marque and Reprisal, coin Money, emit Bills of Credit; make any Thing but gold and silver Coin a Tender in Payment of Debts; pass any Bill of Attainder, ex post facto Law, or Law impairing the Obligation of Contracts, or grant any Title of Nobility.

Express limitations on states

[2]No State shall, without the Consent of the Congress, lay any Imposts or Duties on Imports or Exports, except what may be absolutely necessary for executing its inspection Laws: and the net Produce of all Duties and Imposts, laid by any State on Imports or Exports, shall be for the Use of the Treasury of the United States; and all such Laws shall be subject to the Revision and Control of the Congress.

[3]No State shall, without the Consent of Congress, lay any Duty of Tonnage, keep Troops, or Ships of War in time of Peace, enter into any Agreement or Compact with another State, or with a foreign Power, or engage in War, unless actually invaded, or in such imminent Danger as will not admit of delay.

---

* See also the Sixteenth Amendment.

ARTICLE II • EXECUTIVE DEPARTMENT

Executive power vested in President; term of office— see Twenty-second Amendment

Selection of Presidential electors and number Per state

Obsolete

SECTION 1. [1]The executive Power shall be vested in a President of the United States of America. He shall hold his Office during the Term of four Years, and, together with the Vice President, chosen for the same Term, be elected as follows:

[2]Each State shall appoint, in such Manner as the Legislature thereof may direct, a Number of Electors, equal to the whole Number of Senators and Representatives to which the State may be entitled in the Congress: but no Senator or Representative, or Person holding an Office of Trust or Profit under the United States, shall be appointed an Elector.

[The Electors shall meet in their respective States, and vote by Ballot for two Persons, of whom one at least shall not be an Inhabitant of the same State with themselves. And they shall make a List of all the Persons voted for, and of the Number of Votes for each; which List they shall sign and certify, and transmit sealed to the Seat of the Government of the United States, directed to the President of the Senate. The President of the Senate shall, in the Presence of the Senate and House of Representatives, open all the Certificates, and the Votes shall then be counted. The Person having the greatest Number of Votes shall be the President, if such Number be a Majority of the whole Number of Electors appointed; and if there be more than one who have such Majority, and have an equal Number of Votes, then the House of Representatives shall immediately choose by Ballot one of them for President; and if no Person have a Majority, then from the five highest on the List the said House shall in like Manner choose the President. But in choosing the President, the Votes shall be taken by States, the Representation from each State having one Vote; A quorum for this Purpose shall consist of a Member or Members from two thirds of the States, and a Majority of all the States shall be necessary to a Choice. In every Case, after the Choice of the President, the Person having the greatest Number of Votes of the Electors shall be the Vice President. But if there should remain two or more who have equal Votes, the Senate shall choose from them by Ballot the Vice President.]*

Congress to determine the time of choosing electors and the casting of electoral votes

Required qualifications of President

Succession to the Presidency; also see the Twenty-fifth Amendment

[3]The Congress may determine the Time of choosing the Electors, and the Day on which they shall give their Votes; which Day shall be the same throughout the United States.

[4]No Person except a natural born Citizen, or a Citizen of the United States, at the time of the Adoption of this Constitution, shall be eligible to the Office of President; neither shall any Person be eligible to that Office who shall not have attained to the Age of thirty five Years, and been fourteen Years a Resident within the United States.

[5]In Case of the Removal of the President from Office, or of his Death, Resignation, or Inability to discharge the Powers and Duties of the said Office, the Same shall devolve on the Vice President, and the Congress may by law provide for the Case of Removal, Death, Resignation or Inability, both of the President and Vice President declaring what Officer shall then act as President, and such Officer shall act accordingly, until the Disability be removed, or a President shall be elected.

---

* This paragraph has been superseded by the Twelfth Amendment.

[6]The President shall, at stated Times, receive for his Services, a Compensation, which shall neither be increased nor diminished during the Period for which he shall have been elected, and he shall not receive within that Period any other Emolument from the United States, or any of them.

[7]Before he enter on the Execution of his Office, he shall take the following Oath or Affirmation: "I do solemnly swear (or affirm) that I will faithfully execute the Office of President of the United States, and will to the best of my Ability, preserve, protect and defend the Constitution of the United States."

SECTION 2.   [1]The President shall be Commander in Chief of the Army and Navy of the United States, and of the Militia of the several States, when called into the actual Service of the United States; he may require the Opinion, in writing, of the principal Officer in each of the executive Departments, upon any Subject relating to the Duties of their respective Offices, and he shall have Power to grant Reprieves and Pardons for Offenses against the United States, except in Cases of Impeachment.

[2]He shall have Power, by and with the Advice and Consent of the Senate, to make Treaties, provided two thirds of the Senators present concur; and he shall nominate, and by and with the Advice and Consent of the Senate, shall appoint Ambassadors, other public Ministers and Consuls, Judges of the supreme Court, and all other Officers of the United States, whose Appointments are not herein otherwise provided for, and which shall be established by Law: but the Congress may by Law vest the Appointment of such inferior Officers, as they think proper, in the President alone, in the Courts of Law, or in the Heads of Departments.

[3]The President shall have Power to fill up all Vacancies that may happen during the Recess of the Senate, by granting Commissions which shall expire at the End of their next Session.

SECTION 3.   He shall from time to time give to the Congress Information of the State of the Union, and recommend to their Consideration such Measures as he shall judge necessary and expedient; he may, on extraordinary Occasions, convene both Houses, or either of them, and in Case of Disagreement between them, with Respect to the Time of Adjournment, he may adjourn them to such Time as he shall think proper; he shall receive Ambassadors and other public Ministers; he shall take Care that the Laws be faithfully executed, and shall Commission all the Officers of the United States.

SECTION 4.   The President, Vice President and all civil Officers of the United States, shall be removed from Office on Impeachment for, and Conviction of, Treason, Bribery, or other high Crimes and Misdemeanors.

Compensation of the President

Presidential oath of office

Powers of the President: Commander in Chief

Granting of pardons and reprieves

Treaty-making with advice and consent of Senate

Appointment of officials with advice and consent of Senate; appointment of inferior officers by President alone if Congress so provides

Temporary filling of vacancies

Make recommendations to Congress and provide information

Call special sessions of Congress

Receive ambassadors and other public ministers

Enforce the laws

Civil officers, including President and Vice President, to be removed from office if impeached and convicted

ARTICLE III • JUDICIAL DEPARTMENT

Structure of national judiciary

Tenure and compensation of judges

SECTION 1.   The judicial Power of the United States, shall be vested in one supreme Court, and in such inferior Courts as the Congress may from time to time ordain and establish. The Judges, both of the supreme and inferior Courts, shall hold their Offices during good Behaviour, and shall, at stated Times, receive for their Services, a Compensation, which shall not be diminished during their Continuance in Office.

Jurisdiction of the national judiciary

SECTION 2.   [1]The judicial Power shall extend to all Cases, in Law and Equity, arising under this Constitution, the Laws of the United States; and Treaties made, or which shall be made, under their Authority;—to all Cases affecting Ambassadors, other public Ministers and Consuls;—to all Cases of admiralty and maritime Jurisdiction;—to Controversies to which the United States shall be a Party;—to Controversies between two or more States;—between a State and Citizens of another State;*—between Citizens of different States—between Citizens of the same State claiming Lands under Grants of different States, and between a State, or the Citizens thereof, and foreign States, Citizens or Subjects.

Original and appellate jurisdiction of the Supreme Court

[2]In all Cases affecting Ambassadors, other public Ministers and Consuls, and those in which a State shall be Party, the supreme Court shall have original Jurisdiction. In all the other Cases before mentioned, the supreme Court shall have appellate Jurisdiction, both as to Law and Fact, with such Exceptions, and under such Regulations as the Congress shall make.

Jury trial in criminal cases other than impeachment

[3]The Trial of all Crimes, except in Cases of Impeachment, shall be by Jury; and such Trial shall be held in the State where the said Crimes shall have been committed; but when not committed within any State, the Trial shall be at such Place or Places as the Congress may by Law have directed.

Definition of treason and requisites for conviction

SECTION 3.   [1]Treason against the United States, shall consist only in levying War against them, or in adhering to their Enemies, giving them Aid and Comfort. No Person shall be convicted of Treason unless on the Testimony of two Witnesses to the same overt Act, or on Confession in open Court.

Punishment for treason

[2]The Congress shall have Power to declare the Punishment of Treason, but no Attainder of Treason shall work Corruption of Blood, or Forfeiture except during the Life of the Person attainted.

ARTICLE IV • RELATION OF THE STATES TO EACH OTHER

Interstate obligations: full faith and credit, privileges and immunities of citizens, rendition of fugitives from justice

SECTION 1.   Full Faith and Credit shall be given in each State to the public Acts, Records, and judicial Proceedings of every other State. And the Congress may by general Laws prescribe the Manner in which such Acts, Records and Proceedings shall be proved, and the Effect thereof.

SECTION 2.   [1]The Citizens of each State shall be entitled to all Privileges and Immunities of Citizens in the several States.

[2]A Person charged in any State with Treason, Felony, or other Crime, who shall flee from Justice, and be found in another State, shall on Demand of the executive

---

* This clause has been affected by the Eleventh Amendment.

Authority of the State from which he fled, be delivered up, to be removed to the State having Jurisdiction of the Crime.

[3][No Person held to Service or Labor in one State, under the Laws thereof, escaping into another, shall, in Consequence of any Law or Regulation therein, be discharged from such Service or Labor but shall be delivered up on Claim of the Party to whom such Service or Labor may be due.]*

Obsolete

SECTION 3.   [1]New States may be admitted by Congress into this Union; but no new State shall be formed or erected within the Jurisdiction of any other State; nor any State be formed by the Junction of two or more States, or Parts of States, without the Consent of the Legislature of the States concerned as well as the Congress.

Admission of new states

[2]The Congress shall have Power to dispose of and make all needful Rules and Regulations respecting the Territory or other Property belonging to the United States; and nothing in this Constitution shall be so construed as to Prejudice any Claims of the United States, or of any particular State.

Government of territories

SECTION 4.   The United States shall guarantee to every State in this Union a Republican Form of Government, and shall protect each of them against Invasion; and on Application of the Legislature, or of the Executive (when the Legislature cannot be convened) against domestic Violence.

Guarantee of a republican form of government and protection against invasion and domestic violence

ARTICLE V • AMENDMENTS

The Congress, whenever two thirds of both Houses shall deem it necessary, shall propose Amendments to this Constitution, or, on the Application of the Legislatures of two thirds of the several States, shall call a Convention for proposing Amendments, which, in either Case, shall be valid to all Intents and Purposes, as Part of this Constitution, when ratified by the Legislatures of three fourths of the several States, or by Conventions in three fourths thereof, as the one or the other Mode of Ratification may be proposed by the Congress; Provided, [that no Amendment which may be made prior to the Year One thousand eight hundred and eight shall in any Manner affect the first and fourth Clauses in the Ninth Section of the first Article; and]** that no State, without its Consent, shall be deprived of its equal Suffrage in the Senate.

Proposal and ratification of amendments

ARTICLE VI • GENERAL PROVISIONS

[1]All Debts contracted and Engagements entered into, before the Adoption of this Constitution, shall be as valid against the United States under this Constitution, as under the Confederation.

Validity of debts contracted prior to adoption of the Constitution

[2]This Constitution, and the Laws of the United States which shall be made in Pursuance thereof; and all Treaties made, or which shall be made, under the Authority of the United States, shall be the supreme Law of the Land; and the Judges in every State shall be bound thereby, any Thing in the Constitution or Laws of any State to the Contrary notwithstanding.

Supremacy of the national constitution, laws, and treaties

---

* This paragraph has been superceded by the Thirteenth Amendment.
** Obsolete.

Oath of office to support Constitution: required of all officials, national and state; no religious qualification

[3]The Senators and Representatives before mentioned, and the Members of the several State Legislatures, and all executive and judicial Officers, both of the United States and of the several States, shall be bound by Oath or Affirmation, to support this Constitution; but no religious Test shall ever be required as a Qualification to any Office or public Trust under the United States.

ARTICLE VII • RATIFICATION OF THE CONSTITUTION

Schedule

The Ratification of the Conventions of nine States, shall be sufficient for the Establishment of this Constitution between the States so ratifying the Same.

DONE in convention by the Unanimous Consent of the States present the Seventeenth Day of September in the Year of our Lord one thousand seven hundred and Eighty seven and of the Independence of the United States of America the Twelfth. IN WITNESS whereof We have hereto subscribed our Names.

George Washington
President and Deputy from Virginia

[Signed also by the deputies of twelve States.]

New Hampshire
John Langdon, Nicholas Gilman

New Jersey
William Livingston, David Brearley, William Paterson, Jonathan Dayton

Massachusetts
Nathaniel Gorham, Rufus King

Pennsylvania
Benjamin Franklin, Robert Morris, Thomas FitzSimons, James Wilson, Thomas Mifflin,George Clymer, Jared Ingersoll, Gouverneur Morris

Connecticut
William Samuel Johnson, Roger Sherman

New York
Alexander Hamilton

Delaware
George Read, John Dickinson, Jacob Broom, Gunning Bedford, Jr., Richard Bassett

North Carolina
William Blount, Hugh Williamson, Richard Dobbs Spaight

South Carolina
John Rutledge, Charles Pinckney, Charles Cotesworth Pinckney, Pierce Butler

Maryland
James McHenry, Daniel Carroll, Dan of St. Thomas Jenifer

Georgia
William Few, Abraham Baldwin

Virginia
John Blair, James Madison, Jr.

Attest: *William Jackson,* Secretary

RATIFICATION OF THE CONSTITUTION

The Constitution was adopted by a convention of the States on September 17, 1787, and was subsequently ratified by the several States, on the following dates: Delaware, December 7, 1787; Pennsylvania, December 12, 1787; New Jersey, December 18, 1787; Georgia, January 2, 1788; Connecticut, January 9, 1788; Massachusetts, February 6, 1788; Maryland, April 28, 1788; South Carolina, May 23, 1788; New Hampshire, June 21, 1788; Virginia, June 25, 1788; New York, July 26, 1788; North Carolina, November 21, 1789; Rhode Island, May 29, 1790.

ARTICLES IN ADDITION TO, AND AMENDMENT OF, THE CONSTITUTION OF THE UNITED STATES OF AMERICA, PROPOSED BY CONGRESS, AND RATIFIED BY THE LEGISLATURES OF THE SEVERAL STATES PURSUANT TO THE FIFTH ARTICLE OF THE ORIGINAL CONSTITUTION

ARTICLE I*

Congress shall make no law respecting an establishment of religion, or prohibiting the free exercise thereof; or abridging the freedom of speech, or of the press; or the right of the people peaceably to assemble, and to petition the Government for a redress of grievances.

Freedom of religion, speech, and assembly

ARTICLE II

A well regulated militia, being necessary to the security of a free state, the right of the people to keep and bear arms, shall not be infringed.

Militia and the right to bear arms

ARTICLE III

No soldier shall, in time of peace be quartered in any house, without the consent of the Owner, nor in time of war, but in a manner to be prescribed by law.

Quartering of soldiers

ARTICLE IV

The right of the people to be secure in their persons, houses, papers, and effects, against unreasonable searches and seizures, shall not be violated, and no Warrants shall issue, but upon probable cause, supported by Oath or affirmation, and particularly describing the place to be searched, and the persons or things to be seized.

Unreasonable searches and seizures prohibited

---

* These articles are commonly referred to as amendments. The first 10 are also called the Bill of Rights.

ARTICLE V

Indictment by grand jury; no double jeopardy; due process of law; no self-incrimination; compensation for taking property

No person shall be held to answer for a capital, or otherwise infamous crime, unless on a presentment or indictment of a Grand Jury, except in cases arising in the land or naval forces, or in the Militia, when in actual service in time of War or public danger; nor shall any person be subject for the same offense to be twice put in jeopardy of life or limb; nor shall be compelled in any criminal case to be a witness against himself, nor be deprived of life, liberty, or property, without due process of law; nor shall private property be taken for public use, without just compensation.

ARTICLE VI

Guarantee of basic procedural rights in criminal prosecutions, e.g., jury trial, confrontation of witnesses

In all criminal prosecutions, the accused shall enjoy the right to a speedy and public trial, by an impartial jury of the State and district wherein the crime shall have been committed, which district shall have been previously ascertained by law, and to be informed of the nature and cause of the accusation; to be confronted with the witnesses against him; to have compulsory process for obtaining Witnesses in his favor, and to have the Assistance of Counsel for his defense.

ARTICLE VII

Jury trial in common law suits

In Suits at common law, where the value in controversy shall exceed twenty dollars, the right of trial by jury shall be preserved, and no fact tried by a jury, shall be otherwise reexamined in any Court of the United States, than according to the rules of the common law.

ARTICLE VIII

Excessive bail or fines, cruel and unusual punishments prohibited

Excessive bail shall not be required, nor excessive fines imposed, nor cruel and unusual punishments inflicted.

ARTICLE IX

Retention of rights by the people

The enumeration in the Constitution, of certain rights, shall not be construed to deny or disparage others retained by the people.

ARTICLE X

Reserved powers of the states

The powers not delegated to the United States by the Constitution nor prohibited by it to the States, are reserved to the States respectively, or to the people.

ARTICLE XI

Immunity of states from suits by citizens or aliens in national courts

The Judicial power of the United States shall not be construed to extend to any suit in law or equity, commenced or prosecuted against one of the United States by Citizens of another State, or by Citizens or Subjects of any Foreign State.

ARTICLE XII

The electors shall meet in their respective states and vote by ballot for President and Vice President, one of whom, at least, shall not be an inhabitation of the same state with themselves; they shall name in their ballots the person voted for as President, and in distinct ballots the person voted for as Vice President, and they shall make distinct lists of all persons voted for as President, and of all persons voted for as Vice President, and of the number of votes for each, which lists they shall sign and certify, and transmit sealed to the seat of the government of the United States, directed to the President of the Senate;—The President of the Senate shall, in presence of the Senate and House of Representatives, open all the certificates and the votes shall then be counted;—The person having the greatest number of votes for President, shall be the President, if such number be a majority of the whole number of Electors appointed; and if no person have such majority, then from the persons having the highest numbers not exceeding three on the list of those voted for as President, the House of Representatives shall choose immediately, by ballot, the President. But in choosing the President, the votes shall be taken by states, the representation from each state having one vote; a quorum for this purpose shall consist of a member or members from two-thirds of the states, and a majority of all the states shall be necessary to a choice. [And if the House of Representatives shall not choose a President whenever the right of choice shall devolve upon them, before the fourth day of March next following, then the Vice President shall act as President, as in the case of the death or other constitutional disability of the President.]* The person having the greatest number of votes as Vice President, shall be the Vice President, if such number be a majority of the whole number of Electors appointed, and if no person have a majority, then from the two highest numbers on the list, the Senate shall choose the Vice President; a quorum for the purpose shall consist of two-thirds of the whole number of Senators, and a majority of the whole number shall be necessary to a choice. But no person constitutionally ineligible to the office of President shall be eligible to that of Vice President of the United States.

Replaces third paragraph of Section 1, Article II. Principal provision requires separate ballots for President and Vice President and a majority electoral vote. Procedure to be followed if no candidate obtains a majority

ARTICLE XIII

SECTION 1.   Neither slavery nor involuntary servitude, except as a punishment for crime whereof the party shall have been duly convicted, shall exist within the United States, or any place subject to their jurisdiction.

Slavery and involuntary servitude prohibited

SECTION 2.   Congress shall have power to enforce this article by appropriate legislation.

---

* The part included in square brackets has been superseded by Section 3 of the Twentieth Amendment.

ARTICLE XIV

Definition of United States and state citizenship; no state abridgment of privileges and immunities of United States citizens; no state denial of due process of law or equal protection of the laws to any person

Apportionment of Representatives among the states according to population, excluding untaxed Indians. Provision for reduction of representation under specified circumstances

Disqualification from office-holding by officials who, having taken an oath to support the Constitution, engage in rebellion against the United States

Validity of public debt incurred for suppressing rebellion not to be questioned. All indebtedness incurred in support of rebellion illegal and void

SECTION 1.   All persons born or naturalized in the United States, and subject to the jurisdiction thereof, are citizens of the United States and the State wherein they reside. No State shall make or enforce any law which shall abridge the privileges or immunities of citizens of the United States; nor shall any State deprive any person of life, liberty, or property, without due process of law; nor deny to any person within its jurisdiction the equal protection of the laws.

SECTION 2.   Representatives shall be apportioned among the several States according to their respective numbers, counting the whole number of persons in each State, excluding Indians not taxed. But when the right to vote at any election for the choice of electors for President and Vice President of the United States, Representatives in Congress, the Executive and Judicial officers of a State, or the members of the Legislature thereof, is denied to any of the male inhabitants of such State, being twenty-one years of age, and citizens of the United States, or in any way abridged, except for participation in rebellion, or other crime, the basis of representation therein shall be reduced in the proportion which the number of such male citizens shall bear to the whole number of male citizens twenty-one years of age in such State.

SECTION 3.   No person shall be a Senator or Representative in Congress, or elector of President and Vice President, or hold any office, civil or military, under the United States, or under any State, who, having previously taken an oath, as a member of Congress, or as an officer of the United States, or as a member of any State legislature, or as an executive or judicial officer of any State, to support the Constitution of the United States, shall have engaged in insurrection or rebellion against the same, or given aid or comfort to the enemies thereof. But Congress may by a vote of two-thirds of each House, remove such disability.

SECTION 4.   The validity of the public debt of the United States, authorized by law, including debts incurred for payment of pensions and bounties for services in suppressing insurrection or rebellion, shall not be questioned. But neither the United States nor any State shall assume or pay any debt or obligation incurred in aid of insurrection or rebellion against the United States, or any claim for the loss of emancipation of any slave; but all such debts, obligations and claims shall be held illegal and void.

SECTION 5.   The Congress shall have power to enforce, by appropriate legislation, the provisions of this article.

ARTICLE XV

SECTION 1.   The right of citizens of the United States to vote shall not be denied or abridged by the United States or by any State on account of race, color, or previous condition of servitude.

SECTION 2.   The Congress shall have power to enforce this article by appropriate legislation.

Right of citizens to vote not to be denied because of race, color, or previous condition of servitude

ARTICLE XVI

The Congress shall have power to lay and collect taxes on incomes, from whatever source derived, without apportionment among the several States, and without regard to any census or enumeration.

Congress empowered to levy income taxes without apportionment among states on a population basis

ARTICLE XVII

The Senate of the United States shall be composed of two Senators from each state, elected by the people thereof, for six years; and each Senator shall have one vote. The electors in each State shall have the qualifications requisite for electors of the most numerous branch of the State legislature.

When vacancies happen in the representation of any State in the Senate, the executive authority of such State shall issue writs of election to fill such vacancies: *Provided*, That the legislature of any State may empower the executive thereof to make temporary appointments until the people fill the vacancies by election as the legislature may direct.

This amendment shall not be so construed as to affect the election or term of any Senator chosen before it becomes valid as part of the Constitution.

Popular election of Senators for six-year term by persons qualified to vote for members of the most numerous branch of the state legislature

Procedure for filling vacancies in Senate

ARTICLE XVIII

SECTION 1.   After one year from the ratification of this article the manufacture, sale, or transportation of intoxicating liquors within, the importation thereof into, or the exportation thereof from the United States and all territory subject to the jurisdiction thereof for beverage purposes is hereby prohibited.

Prohibition Amendment; repealed by Twenty-first Amendment

Section 2.   The Congress and the several States shall have concurrent power to enforce this article by appropriate legislation.

Section 3.   This article shall be inoperative unless it shall have been ratified as an amendment to the Constitution by the legislatures of the several States, as provided in the Constitution, within seven years from the date of the submission hereof to the States by the Congress.*

Obsolete

ARTICLE XIX

The right of citizens of the United States to vote shall not be denied or abridged by the United States or by any State on account of sex.

Congress shall have power to enforce this article by appropriate legislation.

Right of citizens to vote not to be denied because of sex

---

* Repealed by Section 1 of the Twenty-First Amendment.

ARTICLE XX

Ending of terms of President, Vice President, Senators, and Representatives

SECTION 1.   The terms of the President and Vice President shall end at noon on the 20th day of January, and the terms of Senators and Representatives at noon on the 3d day of January, of the years in which such terms would have ended if this article had not been ratified; and the terms of their successors shall then begin.

Beginning of required annual Congressional sessions

SECTION 2.   The Congress shall assemble at least once in every year, and such meeting shall begin at noon on the 3d day of January, unless they shall by law appoint a different day.

Procedure to be followed if President-Elect has died or no President has been chosen or qualified by beginning of the Presidential term. This amendment also deals with other contingencies

SECTION 3.   If, at the time fixed for the beginning of the term of the President, the President elect shall have died, the Vice President elect shall become President. If a President shall not have been chosen before the time fixed for the beginning of his term, or if the President elect shall have failed to qualify, then the Vice President elect shall act as President until a President shall have qualified; and the Congress may by law provide for the case wherein neither a President elect nor a Vice President elect shall have qualified, declaring who shall then act as President, or the manner in which one who is to act shall be selected, and such person shall act accordingly until a President or Vice President shall have qualified.

SECTION 4.   The Congress may by law provide for the case of the death of any of the persons from whom the House of Representatives may choose a President whenever the right of choice shall have devolved upon them, and for the case of the death of any of the persons from whom the Senate may choose a Vice President whenever the right of choice shall have devolved upon them.

SECTION 5.   Sections 1 and 2 shall take effect on the 15th day of October following the ratification of this article.

SECTION 6.   This article shall be inoperative unless it shall have been ratified as an amendment to the Constitution by the legislatures of three-fourths of the several States within seven years from the date of its submission.

ARTICLE XXI

The Eighteenth Amendment establishing prohibition repealed

SECTION 1.   The eighteenth article of amendment to the Constitution of the United States is hereby repealed.

SECTION 2.   The transportation or importation into any State, Territory, or possession of the United States for delivery or use therein of intoxicating liquors, in violation of the laws thereof, is hereby prohibited.

SECTION 3.   This article shall be inoperative unless it shall have been ratified as an amendment to the Constitution by conventions in the several States, as provided in the Constitution, within seven years from the date of the submission hereof to the States by the Congress.

ARTICLE XXII

SECTION 1.   No person shall be elected to the office of the President more than twice, and no person who has held the office of President, or acted as President, for more than two years of a term to which some other person was elected President shall be elected to the office of the President more than once. But this article shall not apply to any person holding the office of President when this Article was proposed by the Congress, and shall not prevent any person who may be holding the office of President, or acting as President, during the term within which this Article becomes operative from holding the office of President or acting as President during the remainder of such term.

No person may be elected to Presidency for more than two terms

SECTION 2.   This article shall be inoperative unless it shall have been ratified as an amendment to the Constitution by the legislatures of three-fourths of the several States within seven years from the date of its submission to the States by the Congress.

ARTICLE XXIII

SECTION 1.   The District constituting the seat of Government of the United States shall appoint in such manner as the Congress may direct:

Allocation of presidential electors to District of Columbia

A number of electors of President and Vice President equal to the whole number of Senators and Representatives in Congress to which the District would be entitled if it were a State, but in no event more than the least populous State; they shall be in addition to those appointed by the States, but they shall be considered, for the purposes of the election of President and Vice President, to be electors appointed by a State; and they shall meet in the District and perform such duties as provided by the twelfth article of amendment.

SECTION 2.   The Congress shall have power to enforce this article by appropriate legislation.

ARTICLE XXIV

SECTION 1.   The right of citizens of the United States to vote in any primary or other election for President or Vice President, for electors for President or Vice President, or for Senator or Representative in Congress, shall not be denied or abridged by the United States or any State by reason of failure to pay any poll tax or other tax.

Right of citizens to vote in national elections not to be denied because of failure to pay taxes

SECTION 2.   The Congress shall have power to enforce this article by appropriate legislation.

ARTICLE XXV

Succession to the Presidency and Vice Presidency in case of vacancies

SECTION 1.   In case of the removal of the President from office or of his death or resignation, the Vice President shall become President.

SECTION 2.   Whenever there is a vacancy in the office of the Vice President, the President shall nominate a Vice President who shall take office upon confirmation by a majority vote of both Houses of Congress.

SECTION 3.   Whenever the President transmits to the President pro tempore of the Senate and the Speaker of the House of Representatives his written declaration that he is unable to discharge the powers and duties of his office, and until he transmits to them a written declaration to the contrary, such powers and duties shall be discharged by the Vice President as Acting President.

Presidential disability: procedure for determining when and for how long disability exists. Vice President to act as President for duration of disability

SECTION 4.   Whenever the Vice President and a majority of either the principal officers of the executive departments or of such other body as Congress may by law provide, transmit to the President pro tempore of the Senate and the Speaker of the House of Representatives their written declaration that the President is unable to discharge the powers and duties of his office, the Vice President shall immediately assume the powers and duties of the office as Acting President.

Thereafter, when the President transmits to the President pro tempore of the Senate and the Speaker of the House of Representatives his written declaration that no inability exists, he shall resume the powers and duties of his office unless the Vice President and a majority of either the principal officers of the executive department or of such other body as Congress may by law provide, transmit within four days to the President pro tempore of the Senate and the Speaker of the House of Representatives their written declaration that the President is unable to discharge the powers and duties of his office. Thereupon Congress shall decide the issue, assembling within forty-eight hours for that purpose if not in session. If the Congress, within twenty-one days after receipt of the latter written declaration, or, if Congress is not in session, within twenty-one days after Congress is required to assemble, determines by two-thirds vote of both Houses that the President is unable to discharge the powers and duties of his office, the Vice President shall continue to discharge the same as Acting President; otherwise, the President shall resume the powers and duties of his office.

ARTICLE XXVI

SECTION 1.   The right of citizens of the United States, who are eighteen years of age or older, to vote shall not be denied or abridged by the United States or by any State on account of age.

Citizens eighteen years or older not be denied suffrage because of age

SECTION 2.   The Congress shall have power to enforce this article by appropriate legislation.

ARTICLE XXVII

No law varying the compensation for the services of the Senators and Representatives shall take effect until an election of Representatives shall have intervened.

Congress may not raise its own pay.

Sample Completed Form N-400

Here is a sample completed Form N-400 for an applicant for naturalization. Her name is Anneta Quinones, and she lives in Brooklyn, New York. After she printed the answers to the questions on the form, she mailed the completed form, which you will find on the following pages, to the USCIS Lockbox Facility, USCIS, P.O. Box 660060, Dallas, TX 75266.

As required, she sent two passport-size color photographs, taken within the last 30 days, and a copy of both sides of her Permanent Resident Card. She also sent a money order for $680 ($595 filing fee plus $85 biometrics services fee) made out to U.S. Department of Homeland Security.

Mrs. Quinones arrived in New York on February 2, 1996 and was eligible for naturalization in 2001, but because of personal problems, she did not apply until 2013.

Except for an absence of eight weeks from the United States, Mrs. Quinones has lived continuously in New York State for many years. On Form N-400, she has printed her address for the last five years and has included information about her trip out of the country.

At the present time, Mrs. Quinones is a nurse, but her limited English-speaking skills when she came to this country made it necessary for her to work as a cook in a restaurant for about two years. Information about her job record for the last five years is included in item 6-B. At the present time she has 19 years of experience in a hospital in Brooklyn.

Aurora Quinones, her daughter, is 15 years old and a high school student. Because she is younger than 18 years old, she will automatically become a citizen when her mother is naturalized. The law states that a child admitted to the United States of America legally becomes a citizen if either parent is a citizen.

OMB No. 1615-0052; Expires 03/31/2013

N-400 Application
for Naturalization

Department of Homeland Security
U.S Citizenship and Immigration Services

Print clearly or type your answers using CAPITAL letters. Failure to print clearly may delay your application. Use black ink.

Part 1. Your Name (*Person applying for naturalization*)

A. Your current legal name.

Family Name (*Last Name*)

QUINONES

Given Name (*First Name*)

ANNETA

Full Middle Name (*If applicable*)

ROSA

B. Your name **exactly** as it appears on your Permanent Resident Card.

Family Name (*Last Name*)

QUINONES

Given Name (*First Name*)

ANNETA

Full Middle Name (*If applicable*)

ROSA

C. If you have ever used other names, provide them below.

Family Name (*Last Name*)	Given Name (*First Name*)	Middle Name
CABRERA	ANNETA	ROSA

D. Name change (*optional*)

Read the Instructions before you decide whether to change your name.

1. Would you like to legally change your name? ☐ Yes ☒ No

2. If "Yes," print the new name you would like to use. Do not use initials or abbreviations when writing your new name.

Family Name (*Last Name*)

Given Name (*First Name*)

Full Middle Name

Write your USCIS A-Number here:

A 212-418-418

For USCIS Use Only

Bar Code	Date Stamp

Remarks

Action Block

Part 2. Information About Your Eligibility (*Check only one*)

I am at least 18 years old **AND**

A. ☒ I have been a lawful permanent resident of the United States for at least five years.

B. ☐ I have been a lawful permanent resident of the United States for at least three years, **and** I have been married to and living with the same U.S. citizen for the last three years, **and** my spouse has been a U.S. citizen for the last three years.

C. ☐ I am applying on the basis of qualifying military service.

D. ☐ Other (*Explain*) _____

Form N-400 (Rev. 03/22/12) Y

Figure 20

Part 3. Information About You

Write your USCIS A-Number here:
A 212-418-418

A. U.S. Social Security Number

081-05-8153

B. Date of Birth *(mm/dd/yyyy)*

05/14/1968

C. Date You Became a Permanent Resident *(mm/dd/yyyy)*

02/02/1996

D. Country of Birth

DOMINICAN REPUBLIC

E. Country of Nationality

DOMINICAN REPUBLIC

F. Are either of your parents U.S. citizens? *(If yes, see instructions)* ☐ Yes ☒ No

G. What is your current marital status? ☐ Single, Never Married ☐ Married ☐ Divorced ☐ Widowed

☐ Marriage Annulled or Other *(Explain)* _____

H. Are you requesting a waiver of the English and/or U.S. History and Government requirements based on a disability or impairment and attaching Form N-648 with your application? ☐ Yes ☒ No

I. Are you requesting an accommodation to the naturalization process because of a disability or impairment? *(See instructions for some examples of accommodations.)* ☐ Yes ☒ No

If you answered "Yes," check the box below that applies:

☐ I am deaf or hearing impaired and need a sign language interpreter who uses the following language: _____

☐ I use a wheelchair.

☐ I am blind or sight impaired.

☐ I will need another type of accommodation. Explain: _____

_____

_____

Part 4. Addresses and Telephone Numbers

A. Home Address - Street Number and Name *(Do **not** write a P.O. Box in this space.)*

1150 MIDWOOD ST.

Apartment Number

3A

City	County	State	ZIP Code	Country
BROOKLYN	KINGS	NY	11225	USA

B. Care of _____

Mailing Address - Street Number and Name *(If different from home address)*

Apartment Number

City	State	ZIP Code	Country

C. Daytime Phone Number *(If any)*

(718)347-8000

Evening Phone Number *(If any)*

(718)439-2000

E-Mail Address *(If any)*

Figure 20 (cont.)

| Part 5. Information for Criminal Records Search | Write your USCIS A-Number here:
A 212-418-418 |

NOTE: The categories below are those required by the FBI. See instructions for more information.

A. Gender

☐ Male   ☒ Female

B. Height

| 5 | Feet | 3 | Inches |

C. Weight

| 123 | Pounds |

D. Are you Hispanic or Latino?   ☒ Yes   ☐ No

E. Race *(Select one or more)*

☒ White   ☐ Asian   ☐ Black or African American   ☐ American Indian or Alaskan Native   ☐ Native Hawaiian or Other Pacific Islander

F. Hair color

☐ Black   ☒ Brown   ☐ Blonde   ☐ Gray   ☐ White   ☐ Red   ☐ Sandy   ☐ Bald (No Hair)

G. Eye color

☒ Brown   ☐ Blue   ☐ Green   ☐ Hazel   ☐ Gray   ☐ Black   ☐ Pink   ☐ Maroon   ☐ Other

Part 6. Information About Your Residence and Employment

A. Where have you lived during the last five years? Begin with where you live now and then list every place you lived for the last five years. If you need more space, use a separate sheet of paper.

Street Number and Name, Apartment Number, City, State, Zip Code, and Country	Dates *(mm/dd/yyyy)*	
	From	To
Current Home Address - Same as Part 4.A	01/15/1998	Present

B. Where have you worked (or, if you were a student, what schools did you attend) during the last five years? Include military service. Begin with your current or latest employer and then list every place you have worked or studied for the last five years. If you need more space, use a separate sheet of paper.

Employer or School Name	Employer or School Address *(Street, City, and State)*	Dates *(mm/dd/yyyy)*		Your Occupation
		From	To	
KINGS COUNTY HOSPITAL	CLARKSSON AVE., BROOKLYN, NY	01/01/1994	PRESENT	PRACTICAL NURSE

Figure 20 (cont.)

Part 7. Time Outside the United States
(Including Trips to Canada, Mexico and the Caribbean Islands)

Write your USCIS A-Number here:
A 212-418-418

A. How many total days did you spend outside of the United States during the past five years? **61** days

B. How many trips of 24 hours or more have you taken outside of the United States during the past five years? **1** trips

C. List below all the trips of 24 hours or more that you have taken outside of the United States since becoming a lawful permanent resident. Begin with your most recent trip. If you need more space, use a separate sheet of paper.

Date You Left the United States *(mm/dd/yyyy)*	Date You Returned to the United States *(mm/dd/yyyy)*	Did Trip Last Six Months or More?		Countries to Which You Traveled	Total Days Out of the United States
07/01/2003	08/30/2003	☐ Yes	☒ No	DOMINICAN REPUBLIC	61
		☐ Yes	☐ No		
		☐ Yes	☐ No		
		☐ Yes	☐ No		
		☐ Yes	☐ No		
		☐ Yes	☐ No		
		☐ Yes	☐ No		
		☐ Yes	☐ No		
		☐ Yes	☐ No		
		☐ Yes	☐ No		

Part 8. Information About Your Marital History

A. How many times have you been married (including annulled marriages)? **1** If you have **never** been married, go to Part 9.

B. If you are now married, give the following information about your spouse:

1. Spouse's Family Name *(Last Name)*
N/A

Given Name *(First Name)*
N/A

Full Middle Name *(If applicable)*
N/A

2. Date of Birth *(mm/dd/yyyy)*
N/A

3. Date of Marriage *(mm/dd/yyyy)*
N/A

4. Spouse's U.S. Social Security #
N/A

5. Home Address - Street Number and Name
N/A

Apartment Number
N/A

City
N/A

State
N/A

Zip Code
N/A

Form N-400 (Rev. 03/22/12) Y Page 4

Figure 20 (cont.)

Part 8. Information About Your Marital History *(Continued)*

Write your USCIS A-Number here:
A 212-418-418

C. Is your spouse a U.S. citizen?   ☐ Yes   ☐ No

D. If your spouse is a U.S. citizen, give the following information:

1. When did your spouse become a U.S. citizen?   ☐ At Birth   ☐ Other

If "Other," give the following information:

2. Date your spouse became a U.S. citizen

N/A

3. Place your spouse became a U.S. citizen *(See instructions)*

N/A

City and State

E. If your spouse is **not** a U.S. citizen, give the following information :

1. Spouse's Country of Citizenship

N/A

2. Spouse's USCIS A- Number *(If applicable)*

A N/A

3. Spouse's Immigration Status

☐ Lawful Permanent Resident   ☐ Other N/A

F. If you were married before, provide the following information about your prior spouse. If you have more than one previous marriage, use a separate sheet of paper to provide the information requested in Questions 1-5 below.

1. Prior Spouse's Family Name *(Last Name)*

QUINONES

Given Name *(First Name)*

JOSE

Full Middle Name *(If applicable)*

N/A

2. Prior Spouse's Immigration Status

☐ U.S. Citizen
☒ Lawful Permanent Resident
☐ Other

3. Date of Marriage *(mm/dd/yyyy)*

03/05/1993

4. Date Marriage Ended *(mm/dd/yyyy)*

09/23/2002

5. How Marriage Ended

☐ Divorce   ☒ Spouse Died   ☐ Other

G. How many times has your current spouse been married (including annulled marriages)? ☐

If your spouse has **ever** been married before, give the following information about **your spouse's** prior marriage.
If your spouse has more than one previous marriage, use a separate sheet(s) of paper to provide the information requested in Questions 1 - 5 below.

1. Prior Spouse's Family Name *(Last Name)*

N/A

Given Name *(First Name)*

N/A

Full Middle Name *(If applicable)*

N/A

2. Prior Spouse's Immigration Status

☐ U.S. Citizen
☐ Lawful Permanent Resident
☐ Other

3. Date of Marriage *(mm/dd/yyyy)*

N/A

4. Date Marriage Ended *(mm/dd/yyyy)*

N/A

5. How Marriage Ended

☐ Divorce   ☐ Spouse Died   ☐ Other

Form N-400 (Rev. 03/22/12) Y Page 5

Figure 20 (cont.)

Part 9. Information About Your Children

Write your USCIS A-Number here:
A 212-418-418

A. How many sons and daughters have you had? For more information on which sons and daughters you should include and how to complete this section, see the Instructions.

1

B. Provide the following information about all of your sons and daughters. If you need more space, use a separate sheet of paper.

Full Name of Son or Daughter	Date of Birth (mm/dd/yyyy)	USCIS A- number (if child has one)	Country of Birth	Current Address (Street, City, State and Country)
AURORA QUINONES	04/29/1998	A NONE	DOM. REP.	WITH ME
		A		
		A		
		A		
		A		
		A		
		A		
		A		

Add Children   Go to continuation page

Part 10. Additional Questions

Answer Questions 1 through 14. If you answer "Yes" to any of these questions, include a written explanation with this form. Your written explanation should (1) explain why your answer was "Yes" and (2) provide any additional information that helps to explain your answer.

A. General Questions.

1. Have you **ever** claimed to be a U.S. citizen *(in writing or any other way)*? ☐ Yes ☒ No

2. Have you **ever** registered to vote in any Federal, State, or local election in the United States? ☐ Yes ☒ No

3. Have you **ever** voted in any Federal, State, or local election in the United States? ☐ Yes ☒ No

4. Since becoming a lawful permanent resident, have you **ever** failed to file a required Federal, State, or local tax return? ☐ Yes ☒ No

5. Do you owe any Federal, State, or local taxes that are overdue? ☐ Yes ☒ No

6. Do you have any title of nobility in any foreign country? ☐ Yes ☒ No

7. Have you ever been declared legally incompetent or been confined to a mental institution within the last five years? ☐ Yes ☒ No

Figure 20 (cont.)

| Part 10. Additional Questions *(Continued)* | Write your USCIS A-Number here:
A 212-418-418 |

B. Affiliations.

8. a   Have you **ever** been a member of or associated with any organization, association, fund foundation, party, club, society, or similar group in the United States or in any other place?   ☒ Yes   ☐ No

b. If you answered "Yes," list the name of each group below. If you need more space, attach the names of the other group(s) on a separate sheet of paper.

Name of Group	Name of Group
1. HOSPITAL EMPLOYEES UNION BROOKLYN, NY	6.
2. PARENT TEACHERS ASSOCIATION BROOKLYN, NY	7.
3.	8.
4.	9.
5.	10.

9. Have you **ever** been a member of or in any way associated *(either directly or indirectly)* with:

   a. The Communist Party?   ☐ Yes   ☒ No

   b. Any other totalitarian party?   ☐ Yes   ☒ No

   c. A terrorist organization?   ☐ Yes   ☒ No

10. Have you **ever** advocated *(either directly or indirectly)* the overthrow of any government by force or violence?   ☐ Yes   ☒ No

11. Have you **ever** persecuted *(either directly or indirectly)* any person because of race, religion, national origin, membership in a particular social group, or political opinion?   ☐ Yes   ☒ No

12. Between March 23, 1933, and May 8, 1945, did you work for or associate in any way *(either directly or indirectly)* with:

   a. The Nazi government of Germany?   ☐ Yes   ☒ No

   b. Any government in any area (1) occupied by, (2) allied with, or (3) established with the help of the Nazi government of Germany?   ☐ Yes   ☒ No

   c. Any German, Nazi, or S.S. military unit, paramilitary unit, self-defense unit, vigilante unit, citizen unit, police unit, government agency or office, extermination camp, concentration camp, prisoner of war camp, prison, labor camp, or transit camp?   ☐ Yes   ☒ No

C. Continuous Residence.

Since becoming a lawful permanent resident of the United States:

13. Have you **ever** called yourself a "nonresident" on a Federal, State, or local tax return?   ☐ Yes   ☒ No

14. Have you **ever** failed to file a Federal, State, or local tax return because you considered yourself to be a "nonresident"?   ☐ Yes   ☒ No

Figure 20 (cont.)

Part 10. Additional Questions *(continued)*	Write your USCIS A-Number here: A 212-418-418

D. Good Moral Character.

For the purposes of this application, you must answer "Yes" to the following questions, if applicable, even if your records were sealed or otherwise cleared or if anyone, including a judge, law enforcement officer, or attorney, told you that you no longer have a record.

15. Have you **ever** committed a crime or offense for which you were **not** arrested? ☐ Yes ☒ No

16. Have you **ever** been arrested, cited, or detained by any law enforcement officer (including USCIS or former INS and military officers) for any reason? ☐ Yes ☒ No

17. Have you **ever** been charged with committing any crime or offense? ☐ Yes ☒ No

18. Have you **ever** been convicted of a crime or offense? ☐ Yes ☒ No

19. Have you **ever** been placed in an alternative sentencing or a rehabilitative program (for example: diversion, deferred prosecution, withheld adjudication, deferred adjudication)? ☐ Yes ☒ No

20. Have you **ever** received a suspended sentence, been placed on probation, or been paroled? ☐ Yes ☒ No

21. Have you **ever** been in jail or prison? ☐ Yes ☒ No

If you answered "Yes" to any of Questions 15 through 21, complete the following table. If you need more space, use a separate sheet of paper to give the same information.

Why were you arrested, cited, detained, or charged?	Date arrested, cited, detained, or charged? *(mm/dd/yyyy)*	Where were you arrested, cited, detained, or charged? *(City, State, Country)*	Outcome or disposition of the arrest, citation, detention, or charge *(No charges filed, charges dismissed, jail, probation, etc.)*

Answer Questions 22 through 33. If you answer "Yes" to any of these questions, attach (1) your written explanation why your answer was "Yes" and (2) any additional information or documentation that helps explain your answer.

22. Have you **ever**:

    a. Been a habitual drunkard? ☐ Yes ☒ No

    b. Been a prostitute, or procured anyone for prostitution? ☐ Yes ☒ No

    c. Sold or smuggled controlled substances, illegal drugs, or narcotics? ☐ Yes ☒ No

    d. Been married to more than one person at the same time? ☐ Yes ☒ No

    e. Helped anyone enter or try to enter the United States illegally? ☐ Yes ☒ No

    f. Gambled illegally or received income from illegal gambling? ☐ Yes ☒ No

    g. Failed to support your dependents or to pay alimony? ☐ Yes ☒ No

23. Have you **ever** given false or misleading information to any U.S. Government official while applying for any immigration benefit or to prevent deportation, exclusion, or removal? ☐ Yes ☒ No

24. Have you **ever** lied to any U.S. Government official to gain entry or admission into the United States? ☐ Yes ☒ No

Figure 20 (cont.)

Part 10. Additional Questions *(Continued)*	Write your USCIS A-Number here: A 212-418-418

E. Removal, Exclusion, and Deportation Proceedings.

25. Are removal, exclusion, rescission, or deportation proceedings pending against you? ☐ Yes ☒ No

26. Have you **ever** been removed, excluded, or deported from the United States? ☐ Yes ☒ No

27. Have you **ever** been ordered to be removed, excluded, or deported from the United States? ☐ Yes ☒ No

28. Have you **ever** applied for any kind of relief from removal, exclusion, or deportation? ☐ Yes ☒ No

F. Military Service.

29. Have you **ever** served in the U.S. Armed Forces? ☐ Yes ☒ No

30. Have you **ever** left the United States to avoid being drafted into the U.S. Armed Forces? ☐ Yes ☒ No

31. Have you **ever** applied for any kind of exemption from military service in the U.S. Armed Forces? ☐ Yes ☒ No

32. Have you **ever** deserted from the U.S. Armed Forces? ☐ Yes ☒ No

G. Selective Service Registration.

33. Are you a male who lived in the United States at any time between your 18th and 26th birthdays in any status except as a lawful nonimmigrant? ☐ Yes ☒ No

If you answered "NO," go on to question 34.

If you answered "YES," provide the information below.

If you answered "YES," but you did not register with the Selective Service System and are still under 26 years of age, you must register before you apply for naturalization, so that you can complete the information below:

Date Registered (mm/dd/yyyy) [   ]   Selective Service Number [   ]

If you answered "YES," but you did not register with the Selective Service and you are now 26 years old or older, attach a statement explaining why you did not register.

H. Oath Requirements. *(See Part 14 for the text of the oath)*

Answer Questions 34 through 39. If you answer "No" to any of these questions, attach (1) your written explanation why the answer was "No" and (2) any additional information or documentation that helps to explain your answer.

34. Do you support the Constitution and form of government of the United States? ☒ Yes ☐ No

35. Do you understand the full Oath of Allegiance to the United States? ☒ Yes ☐ No

36. Are you willing to take the full Oath of Allegiance to the United States? ☒ Yes ☐ No

37. If the law requires it, are you willing to bear arms on behalf of the United States? ☒ Yes ☐ No

38. If the law requires it, are you willing to perform noncombatant services in the U.S. Armed Forces? ☒ Yes ☐ No

39. If the law requires it, are you willing to perform work of national importance under civilian direction? ☒ Yes ☐ No

Figure 20 (cont.)

Part 11. Your Signature

Write your USCIS A-Number here:
A 212-418-418

I certify, under penalty of perjury under the laws of the United States of America, that this application, and the evidence submitted with it, are all true and correct. I authorize the release of any information that the USCIS needs to determine my eligibility for naturalization.

Your Signature

Date *(mm/dd/yyyy)*

03/31/2013

Part 12. Signature of Person Who Prepared This Application for You *(If applicable)*

I declare under penalty of perjury that I prepared this application at the request of the above person. The answers provided are based on information of which I have personal knowledge and/or were provided to me by the above named person in response to the *exact questions* contained on this form.

Preparer's Printed Name

Preparer's Signature

Date *(mm/dd/yyyy)*

Preparer's Firm or Organization Name *(If applicable)*

Preparer's Daytime Phone Number

Preparer's Address - Street Number and Name

City

State

Zip Code

NOTE: Do not complete Parts 13 and 14 until a USCIS Officer instructs you to do so.

Part 13. Signature at Interview

I swear (affirm) and certify under penalty of perjury under the laws of the United States of America that I know that the contents of this application for naturalization subscribed by me, including corrections numbered 1 through _____ and the evidence submitted by me numbered pages 1 through _____ , are true and correct to the best of my knowledge and belief.

Subscribed to and sworn to (affirmed) before me

Officer's Printed Name or Stamp

Date *(mm/dd/yyyy)*

Complete Signature of Applicant

Officer's Signature

Part 14. Oath of Allegiance

If your application is approved, you will be scheduled for a public oath ceremony at which time you will be required to take the following Oath of Allegiance immediately prior to becoming a naturalized citizen. By signing, you acknowledge your willingness and ability to take this oath:

I hereby declare, on oath, that I absolutely and entirely renounce and abjure all allegiance and fidelity to any foreign prince, potentate, state, or sovereignty, of whom or which I have heretofore been a subject or citizen;

that I will support and defend the Constitution and laws of the United States of America against all enemies, foreign and domestic;

that I will bear true faith and allegiance to the same;

that I will bear arms on behalf of the United States when required by the law;

that I will perform noncombatant service in the Armed Forces of the United States when required by the law;

that I will perform work of national importance under civilian direction when required by the law; and

that I take this obligation freely, without any mental reservation or purpose of evasion, so help me God.

Printed Name of Applicant

Complete Signature of Applicant

Form N-400 (Rev. 03/22/12) Y Page 10

Figure 20 (cont.)

Exceptions to the General Requirements for Naturalization*

SPECIAL REQUIREMENTS FOR MILITARY PERSONNEL

- ### Current and Recently Discharged U.S. Armed Forces Personnel

If you are in the U.S. armed forces now (or were honorably discharged less than six months ago) **and** you have served for at least one year, you are *exempt* from the following requirements:

- The age requirement
- The continuous residence requirement
- The physical presence requirement—The requirement that you have been physically present in the United States for a certain length of time
- The requirement that you have lived in the state or USCIS district where you are applying for three months

You still are required to demonstrate good moral character; knowledge of English, U.S. history, and civics; and attachment to the Constitution. And you must be a legal permanent resident on the day of your interview.

If you were discharged more than six months prior to submitting your application, or if you served for less than one year, then the general rules for age, continuous residence, physical presence, and residence in the state or USCIS district apply to you.

- ### Military Service During Specified Periods of Conflict

If you performed active duty military service during certain specified periods, you are *exempt* from all the requirements *except* good moral character; knowledge of English, U.S. history, and civics; and attachment to the Constitution. These periods are

- November 11, 1916–April 6, 1917 (World War I)
- September 1, 1939–December 31, 1946 (World War II)

---

*Immigration law is complex and easy to misunderstand. Before submitting an N-400 to apply for citizenship, you should consult with an immigration attorney or a BIA accredited representative. You can find a list of BIA recognized organizations and BIA accredited representatives at *http://www.justice.gov/eoir/ra/raroster.htm*.

- June 25, 1950–July 1, 1955 (Korean Conflict)
- February 28, 1961–October 15, 1978 (Vietnam War)
- August 2, 1990–April 11, 1991 (Persian Gulf War)
- On or after September 11, 2001

- ### Widows or Widowers of U.S. Armed Forces Personnel

If you are at least 18 years of age and were married to and living with a U.S. citizen who died during a period of honorable active-duty service in the U.S. armed forces, you must be a legal permanent resident on the day of your interview, but you are *exempt* from the following requirements:

- The continuous residence requirement
- The physical presence requirement
- The requirement for residence in a state or USCIS district

You still are required to demonstrate good moral character; knowledge of English, U.S. history, and civics; and attachment to the Constitution.

For more information about the special provisions for military personnel, you may request Naturalization Information for Military Personnel (Form M-599) from the USCIS Forms Line at 1-800-870-3676 or online at http://uscis.gov.

OTHER SPECIAL CASES

- ### Service on a Vessel

If you are at least 18 years old and serving on a vessel operated by the United States **or** registered in the United States and owned by U.S. citizens or a U.S. corporation, you must meet all the general requirements for naturalization with the following two exceptions:

- Continuous Residence: Time outside the country while serving on the vessel does not break your continuous residence. It is treated just like time spent in the United States.
- Physical Presence: Time served on the vessel counts as time "physically present" in the United States no matter where you were.

- ### Employees or Contract Employees of the U.S. Government

If you are at least 18 years old and an employee or an individual under contract to the U.S. government, you must meet all the general requirements for naturalization with these two exceptions:

- Continuous Residence: An absence from the United States of one year or more would usually break your continuous residence. However, if you have had at least one year of unbroken continuous residence since becoming a permanent resident and you get an approved Form N-470 before you have been outside the United States for one year, you may keep your continuous residence.

- Physical Presence: Time spent in this type of employment counts as time physically present in the United States no matter where you are as long as you get an approved Form N-470 before you have been outside the United States for one year.

- ## Persons Who Perform Religious Functions

   If you are at least 18 years old and perform ministerial or priestly functions for a religious denomination or an interdenominational organization with a valid presence in the United States, you must meet all the general requirements for naturalization with these two exceptions:

- Continuous Residence: An absence from the United States of one year or more would usually break your continuous residence. However, if you have had at least one year of unbroken continuous residence since becoming a permanent resident and you get an approved Form N-470 before you have been outside the United States for one year, you may keep your continuous residence.
- Physical Presence: Time spent in this type of employment counts as time physically present in the United States no matter where you are as long as you get an approved Form N-470 before you apply for naturalization.

- ## Employees of Certain Nonprofit Organizations

   If you are at least 18 years old and have been employed by a U.S. nonprofit organization that principally promotes the interests of the United States abroad through the communications media, you must have five years as a lawful permanent resident, but you are not required to meet the continuous residence, physical presence, or time in a state or USCIS district requirements. You must meet the other requirements (good moral character; knowledge of English, U.S. history, and civics; and attachment to the Constitution).

- ## Employees of Other American and International Organizations

   If you are at least 18 years old and are employed by one of the following:

- An American institution of research recognized by the attorney general
- An American-owned firm or corporation engaged in the development of foreign trade and commerce for the United States
- A public international organization of which the United States is a member by law or treaty (if the employment began after you became a Permanent Resident)

you must meet all the general requirements for naturalization with the exception of the continuous residence requirement. An absence from the United States of one year or more would usually break your continuous residence. However, if you have had at least one year of unbroken continuous residence since becoming a permanent resident and you get an approved Form N-470 before you have been outside the United States for one year, you may keep your continuous residence.

• <u>Spouses of U.S. Citizens Working Abroad</u>

If you are at least 18 years old and are the spouse of a U.S. citizen who is one of the following:

- A member of the U.S. armed forces
- An employee or an individual under contract to the U.S. government
- An employee of an American institution of research recognized by the attorney general
- An employee of an American-owned firm or corporation engaged in the development of foreign trade and commerce for the United States
- An employee of a public international organization of which the United States is a member by law or treaty
- A person who performs ministerial or priestly functions for a religious denomination or an interdenominational organization with a valid presence in the United States

and you will be proceeding to join your spouse whose work abroad under orders of the qualifying employer will continue for at least one year after the date you will be naturalized, you must be a permanent resident at the time of your USCIS interview, but you do not have to meet the continuous residence, physical presence, or time in state or USCIS district requirements. However, you must be able to demonstrate good moral character; knowledge of English, U.S. history, and civics; and attachment to the Constitution.

You should file Form N-400 before departing.

Answer Key

The Flag

Page 5

1. Red, white, and blue.

2. Red for courage, white for truth, blue for honor.

3. Because there were 13 original colonies.

4. Because each star represents a state.

5. "Star-Spangled Banner"

Citizenship

Review pages 7–8

1. Moving from one place to another.

2. About 40 million.

3. The Immigration Act of 1996.

4. 1899.

5. 1600s.

Review page 9

1–5. See Word List, pages 117–127.

6. a. Alien.

   b. Easy.

7. Easy.

8. A citizen.

9. Being part of the government of the United States is a benefit of citizenship.

10. Being able to vote is a citizen's right.

Review pages 10–11

1–8. See Word List, pages 117–127.

9. In a U.S. courtroom.

10. The Oath of Allegiance is a pledge of loyalty to the United States.

11. To live here and to be part of the country.

12. Yes.

13. No.

Review pages 12–14

1–6. See Word List, pages 117–127.

7. The Constitution.

8. 27

9. The Fourteenth Amendment.

10. They are the rights to life, liberty, and property. No matter where I live, these rights cannot be taken away without due process of law.

11. Liberty.

Quiz pages 14–15

1–7. See Word List, pages 117–127.

8. No.

9. To obey the laws, to know what is going on, to vote, to serve on a jury.

10. To have a voice in government.

11. To make it possible for persons to have a fair trial.

12. To be loyal to the Constitution and government, to obey the laws, to vote, to defend the country, to serve on a jury.

Test page 16

1. You must be at least 18 years old.

2. Yes. Military personnel may be exempt from this requirement (see pages 177 and 178).

3. Marriage to a citizen.

4. Yes. The USCIS may excuse you from this requirement based on physical or mental disability.

Step 2—Civics, History, and Geography

Review page 68

1. Constitution.

2. We the People.

3. Ratified.

4. 13

5. Colonies.

6. Americans.

7. They would have to present the idea to a member of Congress who could introduce it as a bill. If it is passed by a two-thirds vote in both houses, it could be sent to the 50 states for ratification. Three-quarters of the state legislatures would have to ratify before it could become part of the Constitution.

Review page 70

1. The Bill of Rights.

2. Speech, religion, press. It protects the rights to assemble peacefully and to petition the government.

Review pages 71–72

1–8. See Word List, pages 117–127.

9. Checks and balances, separation of powers.

10. Legislative, Senate, House of Representatives.

11. Executive.

12. Vice president.

13. Judicial, interprets.

Review page 74

1–6. See Word List, pages 117–127.

7. One represents the 50 states, the other, the people of the state.

8. No.

9. January 3.

10. When members vote to adjourn, or close, the session.

11. Read page 77.

12. The committee system was devised to make the work of Congress easier.

Review page 80

1–9. See Word List, pages 117–127.

10. To carry out the laws.

11. Many responsibilities.

12. The Cabinet.

13. No.

14. He takes the Presidential Oath of Office at his inauguration.

Review pages 86–88

1–4. See Word List, pages 117–127.

5. To interpret the laws.

6. Supreme Court.

7. Eight associate justices and one chief justice are all appointed by the president.

8. John Roberts.

9. Yes.

10. c

11. c

12. a

13. d

Review page 90

1–8. See Word List, pages 117–127.

9. The Tenth Amendment provides this right.

Review pages 94–95

1–5. See Word List, pages 117–127.

6. *because* these are the colors of the flag.

7. *because* there were 13 states in the beginning.

8. *because* there are 50 states today.

9. *because* they were part of Britain.

10. *because* the flag was adopted on that date in 1777.

The Early Years and the Era of Revolution and Independence

READING EXERCISE #1 pages 100–101

1. American Indians (Native Americans).

2. Any one of the following is correct: freedom, political liberty, religious freedom, economic opportunity, escape persecution.

3. American Indians (Native Americans).

4. Thanksgiving.

5. Any one of the following is correct: because of high taxes, taxation without representation, because the colonists didn't have self-government.

6. Thomas Jefferson.

7. July 4, 1776.

8. Great Britain (or England).

9. Choose any three of the following: New Hampshire, Massachusetts, Rhode Island, Connecticut, New York, New Jersey, Pennsylvania, Delaware, Maryland, Virginia, North Carolina, South Carolina, Georgia.

10. George Washington.

11. George Washington.

12. Either of these is correct: The Constitution was written; the Founding Fathers wrote the Constitution.

13. 1787.

14. Any one of these is correct: James Madison, Alexander Hamilton, John Jay, Publius.

15. Any one of these is correct: U.S. diplomat, oldest member of the constitutional convention, writer of *Poor Richard's Almanac*.

The 1800s

READING EXERCISE #2 page 106

1. Louisiana.

2. Any of these answers is correct: War of 1812, Mexican-American War, Civil War, Spanish-American War.

3. The Civil War *or* the War between the States.

4. Any of these answers is correct: slavery, states' rights, economic reasons.

5. Any of these answers is correct: freed the slaves (Emancipation Proclamation), preserved (saved) the Union, led the Union during the Civil War.

6. Any of these answers is correct: freed the slaves, freed the slaves in the Confederate states, freed the slaves in most southern states.

7. Any of these answers is correct (examiners will have a complete list of the tribes): Cherokee, Navajo, Sioux, Chippewa, Choctaw, Pueblo, Apache, Iroquois, Creek, Blackfeet, Seminole, Cheyenne, Mohegan, Oneida.

8. Fought for women's rights.

Recent American History

READING EXERCISE #3 pages 109–110

1. Any of these answers is correct: World War I, World War II, Korean War, Vietnam War, (Persian) Gulf War.

2. Woodrow Wilson.

3. Franklin Roosevelt.

4. Japan, Germany, and Italy.

5. World War II.

6. Communism.

7. Civil rights movement.

8. Either answer is correct: fought for civil rights, worked for equality for all Americans.

9. Terrorists attacked the United States.

A Glimpse at Geography

READING EXERCISE page 113

1. Adjoining or next to.

2. Pacific Ocean.

3. Atlantic Ocean.

4. Rocky Mountains.

5. All of the following are correct: Maine, New Hampshire, Vermont, New York, Pennsylvania, Ohio, Michigan, Minnesota, North Dakota, Montana, Idaho, Washington, Alaska.

6. All of the following are correct: Texas, New Mexico, Arizona, California.

7. The Mississippi River and the Missouri River.

8. Washington, D.C.

9. Erie, Huron, Ontario, Michigan, Superior.

10. Lake Superior.

11. Any two of the following: Guam, American Samoa, Northern Mariana Islands, U.S. Virgin Islands, Puerto Rico.

12. In New York harbor, on Liberty Island, between the states of New York and New Jersey.

Appendix   American English Idiomatic Expressions

Review pages 133–134

1. used to

2. have time

3. out of the question

4. lay off

5. a little while

6. write away

7. looking forward

8. heard from

9. Bear in mind

10. breakdown

Reading and Writing Vocabulary for the Naturalization Test

U.S. Citizenship
and Immigration
Services

Reading Vocabulary for the Naturalization Test

PEOPLE	CIVICS	PLACES	HOLIDAYS	QUESTION WORDS	VERBS	OTHER (FUNCTION)	OTHER (CONTENT)
Abraham Lincoln	American flag	America	Presidents' Day	How	can	a	colors
George Washington	Bill of Rights	United States	Memorial Day	What	come	for	dollar bill
	capital	U.S.	Flag Day	When	do/does	here	first
	citizen		Independence Day	Where	elects	in	largest
	city		Labor Day	Who	have/has	of	many
	Congress		Columbus Day	Why	is/are/was/be	on	most
	country		Thanksgiving		lives/lived	the	north
	Father of Our Country				meet	to	one
	government				name	we	people
	President				pay		second
	right				vote		south
	Senators				want		
	state/states						
	White House						

(rev. 08/08)

U.S. Citizenship
and Immigration
Services

Writing Vocabulary for the Naturalization Test

PEOPLE	CIVICS	PLACES	MONTHS	HOLIDAYS	VERBS	OTHER (FUNCTION)	OTHER (CONTENT)
Adams	American Indians	Alaska	February	Presidents' Day	can	and	blue
Lincoln	capital	California	May	Memorial Day	come	during	dollar bill
Washington	citizens	Canada	June	Flag Day	elect	for	fifty/50
	Civil War	Delaware	July	Independence Day	have/has	here	first
	Congress	Mexico	September	Labor Day	is/was/be	in	largest
	Father of Our Country	New York City	October	Columbus Day	lives/lived	of	most
	flag	United States	November	Thanksgiving	meets	on	north
	free	Washington			pay	the	one
	freedom of speech	Washington, D.C.			vote	to	one hundred/100
	President				want	we	people
	right						red
	Senators						second
	state/states						south
	White House						taxes
							white

(rev. 08/08)

100 Government, History, and Geography Questions and Their Answers

(rev. 03/11)

U.S. Citizenship and Immigration Services

Civics (History and Government) Questions for the Naturalization Test

The 100 civics (history and government) questions and answers for the naturalization test are listed below. The civics test is an oral test and the USCIS Officer will ask the applicant up to 10 of the 100 civics questions. An applicant must answer 6 out of 10 questions correctly to pass the civics portion of the naturalization test.

On the naturalization test, some answers may change because of elections or appointments. As you study for the test, make sure that you know the most current answers to these questions. Answer these questions with the name of the official who is serving at the time of your eligibility interview with USCIS. The USCIS Officer will not accept an incorrect answer.

Although USCIS is aware that there may be additional correct answers to the 100 civics questions, applicants are encouraged to respond to the civics questions using the answers provided below.

AMERICAN GOVERNMENT

A: Principles of American Democracy

1. **What is the supreme law of the land?**
   - *the Constitution*

2. **What does the Constitution do?**
   - *sets up the government*
   - *defines the government*
   - *protects basic rights of Americans*

3. **The idea of self-government is in the first three words of the Constitution. What are these words?**
   - *We the People*

4. **What is an amendment?**
   - *a change (to the Constitution)*
   - *an addition (to the Constitution)*

5. **What do we call the first ten amendments to the Constitution?**
   - *the Bill of Rights*

6. **What is <u>one</u> right or freedom from the First Amendment?***
   - *speech*
   - *religion*
   - *assembly*
   - *press*
   - *petition the government*

7. **How many amendments does the Constitution have?**
   - *twenty-seven (27)*

* If you are 65 years old or older and have been a legal permanent resident of the United States for 20 or more years, you may study just the questions that have been marked with an asterisk.

8.   **What did the Declaration of Independence do?**
- *announced our independence (from Great Britain)*
- *declared our independence (from Great Britain)*
- *said that the United States is free (from Great Britain)*

9.   **What are <u>two</u> rights in the Declaration of Independence?**
- *life*
- *liberty*
- *pursuit of happiness*

10.   **What is freedom of religion?**
- *You can practice any religion, or not practice a religion.*

11.   **What is the economic system in the United States?***
- *capitalist economy*
- *market economy*

12.   **What is the "rule of law"?**
- *Everyone must follow the law.*
- *Leaders must obey the law.*
- *Government must obey the law.*
- *No one is above the law.*

B: System of Government

13.   **Name <u>one</u> branch or part of the government.***
- *Congress*
- *legislative*
- *President*
- *executive*
- *the courts*
- *judicial*

14.   **What stops <u>one</u> branch of government from becoming too powerful?**
- *checks and balances*
- *separation of powers*

15.   **Who is in charge of the executive branch?**
- *the President*

16.   **Who makes federal laws?**
- *Congress*
- *Senate and House (of Representatives)*
- *(U.S. or national) legislature*

17.   **What are the <u>two</u> parts of the U.S. Congress?***
- *the Senate and House (of Representatives)*

18.   **How many U.S. Senators are there?**
- *one hundred (100)*

* If you are 65 years old or older and have been a legal permanent resident of the United States for 20 or more years, you may study just the questions that have been marked with an asterisk.

19. **We elect a U.S. Senator for how many years?**
    - *six (6)*

20. **Who is <u>one</u> of your state's U.S. Senators now?***
    - *Answers will vary. [District of Columbia residents and residents of U.S. territories should answer that D.C. (or the territory where the applicant lives) has no U.S. Senators.]*

21. **The House of Representatives has how many voting members?**
    - *four hundred thirty-five (435)*

22. **We elect a U.S. Representative for how many years?**
    - *two (2)*

23. **Name your U.S. Representative.**
    - *Answers will vary. [Residents of territories with nonvoting Delegates or Resident Commissioners may provide the name of that Delegate or Commissioner. Also acceptable is any statement that the territory has no (voting) Representatives in Congress.]*

24. **Who does a U.S. Senator represent?**
    - *all people of the state*

25. **Why do some states have more Representatives than other states?**
    - *(because of) the state's population*
    - *(because) they have more people*
    - *(because) some states have more people*

26. **We elect a President for how many years?**
    - *four (4)*

27. **In what month do we vote for President?***
    - *November*

28. **What is the name of the President of the United States now?***
    - *Barack Obama*
    - *Obama*

29. **What is the name of the Vice President of the United States now?**
    - *Joseph R. Biden, Jr.*
    - *Joe Biden*
    - *Biden*

30. **If the President can no longer serve, who becomes President?**
    - *the Vice President*

31. **If both the President and the Vice President can no longer serve, who becomes President?**
    - *the Speaker of the House*

32. **Who is the Commander in Chief of the military?**
    - *the President*

33. **Who signs bills to become laws?**
    - *the President*

34. **Who vetoes bills?**
    - *the President*

---

* If you are 65 years old or older and have been a legal permanent resident of the United States for 20 or more years, you may study just the questions that have been marked with an asterisk.

35. **What does the President's Cabinet do?**
    - *advises the President*

36. **What are <u>two</u> Cabinet-level positions?**
    - *Secretary of Agriculture*
    - *Secretary of Commerce*
    - *Secretary of Defense*
    - *Secretary of Education*
    - *Secretary of Energy*
    - *Secretary of Health and Human Services*
    - *Secretary of Homeland Security*
    - *Secretary of Housing and Urban Development*
    - *Secretary of the Interior*
    - *Secretary of Labor*
    - *Secretary of State*
    - *Secretary of Transportation*
    - *Secretary of the Treasury*
    - *Secretary of Veterans Affairs*
    - *Attorney General*
    - *Vice President*

37. **What does the judicial branch do?**
    - *reviews laws*
    - *explains laws*
    - *resolves disputes (disagreements)*
    - *decides if a law goes against the Constitution*

38. **What is the highest court in the United States?**
    - *the Supreme Court*

39. **How many justices are on the Supreme Court?**
    - *nine (9)*

40. **Who is the Chief Justice of the United States now?**
    - *John Roberts (John G. Roberts, Jr.)*

41. **Under our Constitution, some powers belong to the federal government. What is <u>one</u> power of the federal government?**
    - *to print money*
    - *to declare war*
    - *to create an army*
    - *to make treaties*

42. **Under our Constitution, some powers belong to the states. What is <u>one</u> power of the states?**
    - *provide schooling and education*
    - *provide protection (police)*
    - *provide safety (fire departments)*
    - *give a driver's license*
    - *approve zoning and land use*

* If you are 65 years old or older and have been a legal permanent resident of the United States for 20 or more years, you may study just the questions that have been marked with an asterisk.

43.   **Who is the Governor of your state now?**
- *Answers will vary. [District of Columbia residents should answer that D.C. does not have a Governor.]*

44.   **What is the capital of your state?***
- *Answers will vary. [District of Columbia residents should answer that D.C. is not a state and does not have a capital. Residents of U.S. territories should name the capital of the territory.]*

45.   **What are the <u>two</u> major political parties in the United States?***
- *Democratic and Republican*

46.   **What is the political party of the President now?**
- *Democratic (Party)*

47.   **What is the name of the Speaker of the House of Representatives now?**
- *(John) Boehner*

C: Rights and Responsibilities

48.   **There are four amendments to the Constitution about who can vote. Describe <u>one</u> of them.**
- *Citizens eighteen (18) and older (can vote).*
- *You don't have to pay (a poll tax) to vote.*
- *Any citizen can vote. (Women and men can vote.)*
- *A male citizen of any race (can vote).*

49.   **What is <u>one</u> responsibility that is only for United States citizens?***
- *serve on a jury*
- *vote in a federal election*

50.   **Name <u>one</u> right only for United States citizens.**
- *vote in a federal election*
- *run for federal office*

51.   **What are <u>two</u> rights of everyone living in the United States?**
- *freedom of expression*
- *freedom of speech*
- *freedom of assembly*
- *freedom to petition the government*
- *freedom of worship*
- *the right to bear arms*

52.   **What do we show loyalty to when we say the Pledge of Allegiance?**
- *the United States*
- *the flag*

53.   **What is <u>one</u> promise you make when you become a United States citizen?**
- *give up loyalty to other countries*
- *defend the Constitution and laws of the United States*
- *obey the laws of the United States*
- *serve in the U.S. military (if needed)*
- *serve (do important work for) the nation (if needed)*
- *be loyal to the United States*

* If you are 65 years old or older and have been a legal permanent resident of the United States for 20 or more years, you may study just the questions that have been marked with an asterisk.

54. **How old do citizens have to be to vote for President?***
    - *eighteen (18) and older*

55. **What are <u>two</u> ways that Americans can participate in their democracy?**
    - *vote*
    - *join a political party*
    - *help with a campaign*
    - *join a civic group*
    - *join a community group*
    - *give an elected official your opinion on an issue*
    - *call Senators and Representatives*
    - *publicly support or oppose an issue or policy*
    - *run for office*
    - *write to a newspaper*

56. **When is the last day you can send in federal income tax forms?***
    - *April 15*

57. **When must all men register for the Selective Service?**
    - *at age eighteen (18)*
    - *between eighteen (18) and twenty-six (26)*

AMERICAN HISTORY

A: Colonial Period and Independence

58. **What is <u>one</u> reason colonists came to America?**
    - *freedom*
    - *political liberty*
    - *religious freedom*
    - *economic opportunity*
    - *practice their religion*
    - *escape persecution*

59. **Who lived in America before the Europeans arrived?**
    - *American Indians*
    - *Native Americans*

60. **What group of people was taken to America and sold as slaves?**
    - *Africans*
    - *people from Africa*

61. **Why did the colonists fight the British?**
    - *because of high taxes (taxation without representation)*
    - *because the British army stayed in their houses (boarding, quartering)*
    - *because they didn't have self-government*

62. **Who wrote the Declaration of Independence?**
    - *(Thomas) Jefferson*

* If you are 65 years old or older and have been a legal permanent resident of the United States for 20 or more years, you may study just the questions that have been marked with an asterisk.

63. **When was the Declaration of Independence adopted?**
   - *July 4, 1776*

64. **There were 13 original states. Name <u>three</u>.**
   - *New Hampshire*
   - *Massachusetts*
   - *Rhode Island*
   - *Connecticut*
   - *New York*
   - *New Jersey*
   - *Pennsylvania*
   - *Delaware*
   - *Maryland*
   - *Virginia*
   - *North Carolina*
   - *South Carolina*
   - *Georgia*

65. **What happened at the Constitutional Convention?**
   - *The Constitution was written.*
   - *The Founding Fathers wrote the Constitution.*

66. **When was the Constitution written?**
   - *1787*

67. **The Federalist Papers supported the passage of the U.S. Constitution. Name <u>one</u> of the writers.**
   - *(James) Madison*
   - *(Alexander) Hamilton*
   - *(John) Jay*
   - *Publius*

68. **What is <u>one</u> thing Benjamin Franklin is famous for?**
   - *U.S. diplomat*
   - *oldest member of the Constitutional Convention*
   - *first Postmaster General of the United States*
   - *writer of "Poor Richard's Almanac"*
   - *started the first free libraries*

69. **Who is the "Father of Our Country"?**
   - *(George) Washington*

70. **Who was the first President?***
   - *(George) Washington*

B: 1800s

71. **What territory did the United States buy from France in 1803?**
   - *the Louisiana Territory*
   - *Louisiana*

* If you are 65 years old or older and have been a legal permanent resident of the United States for 20 or more years, you
   may study just the questions that have been marked with an asterisk.

72.   Name <u>one</u> war fought by the United States in the 1800s.
  - *War of 1812*
  - *Mexican-American War*
  - *Civil War*
  - *Spanish-American War*

73.   Name the U.S. war between the North and the South.
  - *the Civil War*
  - *the War between the States*

74.   Name <u>one</u> problem that led to the Civil War.
  - *slavery*
  - *economic reasons*
  - *states' rights*

75.   What was <u>one</u> important thing that Abraham Lincoln did?*
  - *freed the slaves (Emancipation Proclamation)*
  - *saved (or preserved) the Union*
  - *led the United States during the Civil War*

76.   What did the Emancipation Proclamation do?
  - *freed the slaves*
  - *freed slaves in the Confederacy*
  - *freed slaves in the Confederate states*
  - *freed slaves in most Southern states*

77.   What did Susan B. Anthony do?
  - *fought for women's rights*
  - *fought for civil rights*

C: Recent American History and Other Important Historical Information

78.   Name <u>one</u> war fought by the United States in the 1900s.*
  - *World War I*
  - *World War II*
  - *Korean War*
  - *Vietnam War*
  - *(Persian) Gulf War*

79.   Who was President during World War I?
  - *(Woodrow) Wilson*

80.   Who was President during the Great Depression and World War II?
  - *(Franklin) Roosevelt*

81.   Who did the United States fight in World War II?
  - *Japan, Germany, and Italy*

82.   Before he was President, Eisenhower was a general. What war was he in?
  - *World War II*

* If you are 65 years old or older and have been a legal permanent resident of the United States for 20 or more years, you may study just the questions that have been marked with an asterisk.

83. **During the Cold War, what was the main concern of the United States?**
    - *Communism*

84. **What movement tried to end racial discrimination?**
    - *civil rights (movement)*

85. **What did Martin Luther King, Jr. do?***
    - *fought for civil rights*
    - *worked for equality for all Americans*

86. **What major event happened on September 11, 2001, in the United States?**
    - *Terrorists attacked the United States.*

87. **Name one American Indian tribe in the United States.**
    [USCIS Officers will be supplied with a list of federally recognized American Indian tribes.]
    - *Cherokee*
    - *Navajo*
    - *Sioux*
    - *Chippewa*
    - *Choctaw*
    - *Pueblo*
    - *Apache*
    - *Iroquois*
    - *Creek*
    - *Blackfeet*
    - *Seminole*
    - *Cheyenne*
    - *Arawak*
    - *Shawnee*
    - *Mohegan*
    - *Huron*
    - *Oneida*
    - *Lakota*
    - *Crow*
    - *Teton*
    - *Hopi*
    - *Inuit*

INTEGRATED CIVICS

A: Geography

88. **Name one of the two longest rivers in the United States.**
    - *Missouri (River)*
    - *Mississippi (River)*

89. **What ocean is on the West Coast of the United States?**
    - *Pacific (Ocean)*

* If you are 65 years old or older and have been a legal permanent resident of the United States for 20 or more years, you may study just the questions that have been marked with an asterisk.

90. **What ocean is on the East Coast of the United States?**
    - *Atlantic (Ocean)*

91. **Name <u>one</u> U.S. territory.**
    - *Puerto Rico*
    - *U.S. Virgin Islands*
    - *American Samoa*
    - *Northern Mariana Islands*
    - *Guam*

92. **Name <u>one</u> state that borders Canada.**
    - *Maine*
    - *New Hampshire*
    - *Vermont*
    - *New York*
    - *Pennsylvania*
    - *Ohio*
    - *Michigan*
    - *Minnesota*
    - *North Dakota*
    - *Montana*
    - *Idaho*
    - *Washington*
    - *Alaska*

93. **Name <u>one</u> state that borders Mexico.**
    - *California*
    - *Arizona*
    - *New Mexico*
    - *Texas*

94. **What is the capital of the United States?***
    - *Washington, D.C.*

95. **Where is the Statue of Liberty?***
    - *New York (Harbor)*
    - *Liberty Island*

    [Also acceptable are New Jersey, near New York City, and on the Hudson (River).]

B: Symbols

96. **Why does the flag have 13 stripes?**
    - *because there were 13 original colonies*
    - *because the stripes represent the original colonies*

97. **Why does the flag have 50 stars?***
    - *because there is one star for each state*
    - *because each star represents a state*
    - *because there are 50 states*

* If you are 65 years old or older and have been a legal permanent resident of the United States for 20 or more years, you may study just the questions that have been marked with an asterisk.

98. **What is the name of the national anthem?**
    - *The Star-Spangled Banner*

C: Holidays

99. **When do we celebrate Independence Day?***
    - *July 4*

100. **Name two national U.S. holidays.**
    - *New Year's Day*
    - *Martin Luther King, Jr. Day*
    - *Presidents' Day*
    - *Memorial Day*
    - *Independence Day*
    - *Labor Day*
    - *Columbus Day*
    - *Veterans Day*
    - *Thanksgiving*
    - *Christmas*

* If you are 65 years old or older and have been a legal permanent resident of the United States for 20 or more years, you may study just the questions that have been marked with an asterisk.

Index

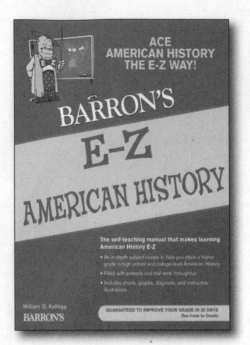
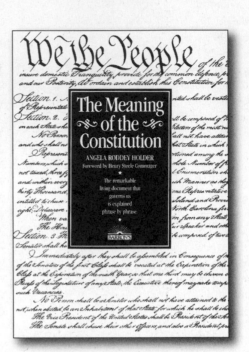